Real Estate Market Analysis The Ultimate Beginner's Guide Book

How To Invest In Real Estate

By : Investing Basics

Published By:

Investing Basics

Table of Contents

Introduction

Are you ready to start discovering the globe of genuine-estate investing? You've concerned the appropriate place, and you may be surprised to learn that the subject could take you down several different pathways. There's a real-estate specialty to suit nearly every person.

You've no uncertainty heard individuals claim, "I desire I had bought realty thirty years back." Well, thirty years from now, people will certainly still be making that comment. There's no time at all like the present to obtain started. The longer you wait, the higher real-estate prices will certainly be-- that's one factor real estate is such a terrific location to invest your money. It's one of one of the most stable assets you'll ever before find. The worst error you can make is not buying the "incorrect" property-- it's denying anything at all. Many real-estate financiers locate that residential properties are the ideal place to begin-- they're a secure investment and, when you decide on wisely, not also challenging to turn around quickly. Whether you adhere to that path or branch off to another is up to you. There's plenty to pick from, including industrial real estate, land advancement, or owning as well as taking care of a huge apartment building or strip mall-- probably one of those specialties is a lot more attractive to you.

You'll become an excellent detective as you discover how to research residential properties and also locate their owners. The real-estate arrangement procedure will aid you enhance your individuals skills since it requires you to communicate with home-buyers, home-sellers, renters, brokers, and other participants of the real-estate area. The understanding you'll obtain will certainly aid you buy and sell personal residences, as well. You'll even get to exercise your home maintenance and repair as well as maintenance talents as you renovate and also look after your assets residential properties-- and who among us cannot make use of those skills each day?

Get ready to discover just how much enjoyable it is to get a piece of realty that everyone else assumes is a catastrophe and also to use your imagination and knowledge of the marketplace to transform it right into a property that's in high demand. Success takes a good bit of creative imagination-- including the ability to see past damaged paint and outdated decorating-- and it requires devotion as well as a desire to get your hands filthy every now and then. It's most definitely worth the effort-- a successful real-estate assets career can put cash in your pocket today as well as aid safeguard your future wide range.

This book offers a detailed analysis of the process of buying, selling, as well as renting real estate. It's essential for you to understand the information that have to be considered before you initiate any sort of sort of real-estate purchase, as well as this publication supplies a solid background to help you do just that.

Some bargains are unsafe-- others are a certainty. Even more threat usually amounts to much more prospective gains (and losses), however several people could still do without the anxiety associated with those purchases. Not to fret, considering that there's a spot for everybody, as well as locating it can be an exciting journey when you have the background you should feel confident regarding your choices. Use the sources on the adhering to pages to assist you locate your particular niche-- that unique section of real estate where each of us has a residence

Chapter 1:
Starting

In time, property has really revealed to be one of the most stable financial investments a person could make. If you do your study and allow good sense quick guide you, the dangers are much less than you'll experience in the stock exchange, nonetheless the gains can be simply as fantastic. Residential property takes initiative as well as dedication, nevertheless if you're prepared to wrap your sleeves and obtain your hands filthy, your initiatives will be rewarded.

Is Real-Estate Investing Right for You?

Prior to you obtain consisted of, consider your goals as well as motivations. Do you would like to rob residential property because you've listened to that it provides quickly revenues with little initiative?

If that's the situation, you might have to rethink your attitude. If buying residential property were a very easy activity with rapid rewards, everybody would certainly be doing it. The majority of individuals which recommend those quickie (and also sometimes doubtful) methods make their revenue from selling their books as well as tapes, not from working in residential property.

Dealing with real estate is initiative that needs a lot of research study prior to you also take into consideration making an offer. The offer itself need to be crafted very carefully in order to safeguard your passions. Arrangements need to be positioned that permit you to back out with no costs if certain conditions are not contented and also you will not comprehend specifically just what arrangements to request unless you've done your study.

After an offer is approved, the job of acquiring the bargain to the closing table. That journey can be filled of a variety of problems:.

- The evaluation might return low.
- An examination may reveal structural issues that you're not going to deal with.
- The level of radon gas may be high, requiring a reduction system to decrease it.
- Your funding supplier could not accept the financing.

There are exceptionally few hassle-free offers, so be pre pared to deal with demanding scenarios, no matter what type of real-estate financial assets you select. Before you start, take a while to examine yourself and your inspirations. Looking at that treatment will absolutely aid you identify precisely where you suit the world of real-estate economic investments.

Consider Where You Fit In

Discovering your specific niche is precisely what it's everything around, isn't truly it? You'll be more effective in your monetary investment career if you genuinely like just what you are doing. If you do not indulge in handling individuals, taking on property owner tasks most likely isn't really for you. You can still have rentals, however intend on having someone else take care of the management. If you could not handle stress and anxiety, do not take care of commercial properties or any property that appears exceptionally risky a minimum of not till you have a great deal of added cash and also positive self-image in your ability to handle all stages of a task.

TRUTH.

Many financiers begin by staying in a financial investment prop erty while they get it readied to offer or rent out. That method provides advantages, consisting of the lower down-payment as well as rate of interest that are available for owner-occupied homes, in addition to one much less home mortgage payment.

Your Available Time.

Just how much time do you have to dedicate to home? The most effective earnings are commonly the result of reconditioning a cosmetically challenged or real fixer-upper residence. The more job you can do on your own, the more money will certainly stay in your pocket when it's time to lease or provide.

Nonetheless, if you already function sixty hours a week, you'll have to collaborate with somebody to manage every re-modeling task. That does not merely lower earnings it often implies it will absolutely take longer to finish the task.

Your Personal Life.

Do you have a spouse, a household, or a better half? How do they really feel regarding sharing you with your real-estate career? An efficient profession in property takes a big amount of time and initiative. When you've made it to some degree, you can hand over responsibilities and utilize help, but for most us that takes some time. It's less complex on your residence life if your delighted in ones have an interest in being associated with some way or are at least understanding of your goals.

Your Hands-On Expectations

You're obtaining your hands unclean. At the very least, intend on doing a large amount of cleaning. Painting is a provided, as well. Just how about laying floor tile and also carpets and taping off dry- wall surface are you roughly those tasks? Otherwise, it will restrict the number of homes you must think about, unless you have someone that will certainly do the work for you for a reason able price.

Your Flair for Interior as well as Exterior Decor

You might be stunned the number of buyers could not see previous dirty floors and scuffed walls. If you desire to be effective in real-estate investing, you should be able to look past the area and also visualize what the framework will certainly look like with a fundamental clean-up, then take it a step further to recognize exactly what type of changes would make substantial enhancements in its look and also use.

An effective method to educate on your own to be able to view the potential in any type of residential property is to look into enhancing publications, take pleasure in home-improvement programs, and browse the Internet for decorating concepts. The more info you're exposed to, the more probable you are to intuitively recognize what ought to be done to make prompt enhancements to a residential property, in and out.

Where Will You Get the Funding?

Do you have set you back savings or access to various other funds? Mortgage terms for economic investment residences aren't as liberal as loans for owner-occupied houses, as well as they're also stricter for commercial financial assets. You may be able to persuade a vendor to money all or a portion of the property, but you'll need cash or a credit line to make updates as well as repair works.

It may be compensating to drift expenditures for jobs you think you could pass on swiftly on a bank card, however you sure do not want to be stuck to a high-interest debt for long. High credit-card equilibriums can also influence the method home loan lenders assess your credit report reports and also scores.

For how long can you handle a negative cash flow just before it harms you economically? Your very first job might go quickly, nonetheless it's more sensible to expect hold-ups. Dealing with real- estate sales and leasings is a figuring out procedure, and also it may take a number of offers prior to your abilities are constant. Plan your budget plan to include provided money for hold-ups and possible issues.

Your Comfort Level

Most especially, consider your comfort degree. The amount of are you about to run the risk of? While it's real that genuine- estate investing is much less harmful than the stock exchange or a lot of company economic assets, the danger components rely on exactly what form of property you're dealing with. Buying domestic realty brings much less risk compared to commercial residential properties and land investments, nonetheless some hazard is still entailed. If you could not take care of any kind of kind of risk in any way, property is not your preferably assets choice.

ISSUE?

Are you going to make sacrifices?

Purchasing an investment home will probably take a bite from your complimentary money, the dollars you utilize to having fun. Are you visiting give that for time? Less suppers out, less trips, a basic cutback on home entertainment is it worth it to you to do away with these points while you establish equity in properties?

Assess Your Real-Estate Market

There are prospective real-estate economic assets of every kind, from single-family residences to huge industrial developments. Exactly what's right for you? Some investors are con camping outdoor tents acquiring and also selling homes. There's lots of diversification during that solitary field because we can focus on repossessions, fixer-uppers, multifamily jobs, or other sorts of residences. Every other place of realty offers just as much wide range, so there's some thing for everyone. The trick is locating the area of the real-estate market that you enjoy the most.

Precisely exactly what's in Demand Close to Home?

Unless you stay in a very town, there are probably various real-estate assets avenues to pursue. The most vital thing you can do is keep your mind open to all opportunities. Look at homes from a fresh viewpoint, visualizing just what they could be with updates or simple alterations rather than focusing on their status quo.

The majority of residences that are available for sale are noted with authentic- estate companies, so the majority of purchasers visit representatives when they are in the marketplace to purchase. Experienced real- estate brokers can be amongst your ideal sources of info about specifically just what customers as well as lessees are searching for. Develop a connection with many reps who specialize in the sorts of homes you wish to purchase.

Check out all your neighborhood files, and also get every actual- estate for-sale magazine that's offered in your community. Pay quite close attention to ads, remembering prices versus features for rental houses and residential properties noted for sale. Take workout drives with the areas you are most thinking about. Your objective is to wind up being experienced about every facet of the real-estate market in your town.

Have a look at regional demographics. Is your customer swimming pool composed mainly of one team of people, such as elderly people? Referred to as long as you could regarding the population make-up will definitely aid you with any sort of type of real-estate investment, from offering single-family homes to uncovering business lessees that concentrate on companies as well as customer services crucial to your community.

National and International Opportunities

If you cannot uncover what you're trying to find in your area, branch out to various other locations. There's never ever been a much better time to go shopping throughout the nation or internationally the Internet brings far-off real-estate possibilities to anyone that has a computer system as well as a Web link.

A drawback of remote financial assets is handling them effectively, so be prepared to work with someone to manage occupants as well as upkeep for you. The added expense must be taken into consideration when you assess the potential re activates your economic investment.

However before you branch out to various other places, it's essential to become familiar with your local real-estate market. Real-estate deals are taken care of exceptionally in different ways across the United States. Worldwide, you'll view far more variations. Recognizing your regional procedure will give you more confidence and also better ready you to ask issues concerning the treatments in various other locations.

One means to start a real-estate monetary investment career at a far-off area is to acquire a villa. Just how around a place where you would like to invest a few weeks each year, or a location where you think you wish to retire? Opportunities are it's a spot you already recognize a minimum of a bit about, which can be a plus when it's time to select homes.

If you have a young person or grandchild far from house in college, consider buying a house or apartment instead of paying lease for a dorm or home. The residence will certainly load a need during the young adult's college years, and also its value will certainly value for you. Make the time away from property an investment opportunity as opposed to paying rental fee for 4 or more years. Market the house when your children leaves institution, or remain to use it as a leasing for various other students

Discovering Your First Investment

Buying a single-family house is a superb approach to begin your real-estate financial investment job. Why should you choose a single-family home? Considering that they are commonly the properties in a lot of requirement, which then makes them the best properties to provide. Allow's walk through a typical scenario, where you've examined the marketplace in preparation to buy a single-family home.

Let's explain your market research reveals that elderly people make up a large part of the buying swimming pool in your town. They likely prefer a property that's not insufficient, nevertheless not also substantial, either. A three-bedroom, two-bath house is most effectively, something around 2,000 square feet or a little less.

Regional agents have actually advised you to search for a home with no actions or just a couple of. Even seniors which aren't bothered by steps yet are seeking one-level living with a minimum of stairs to go up. That removes split-foyer properties, residences where you need to climb up high porches in order to go into the front door, as well as residences with finished living places on 2 levels.

Most seniors want a home in move-in problem. They don't want to repaint or make repair works. That's where you step in. Your objective is to discover a residence that's structurally sound and also has the needed features nevertheless that needs cosmetic updates. If you cannot discover that type of home at a bargain expense, you might have to look at houses that require a little bit much more job, nonetheless for this first purchase, stay away from anything that includes structural repair services unless you are a skilled builder.

ALERT!

Lenders deal lesser rates of interest and down-payment terms for owner-occupied homes, so relocating right into the financial investment home could possibly save you money. If you live there for 2 years or less, you won't also owe funding gains taxes when you provide it. Lots of investors move from home to house, enhancing their gains with each sale. You've chatted with adequate real-estate agents to comprehend that wood floorings are prominent which seniors in your area like gas fireplaces to the wood-burning versions. If you cannot discover a residence with those features, you prepare to add them. You have a wonderful suggestion of our home you want to acquire, so now it's time to start looking.

Check the Neighborhoods.

Your perfect locate is a rather rundown house in a desirable, low-crime area close to shopping, hospitals, and also other customer services. Ask a representative just what's for sale in neighborhoods that match that description, and also acquire copies of many listing sheets to make sure that you'll have addresses and thorough information about your homes. Do not merely drive by those houses search other streets in the exact very same communities to uncover For Sale by Owner (FSBO) properties that representatives won't discuss.

Explore the Properties.

Make consultations to view the most intriguing residential

properties. Remember about inside as well as outside parts. Detail one of the most desirable attributes of each house. What updates are needed? A complete kitchen area overhaul could be costly, yet possibly you could manage with paint or tarnishing the cabinets and bring in brand-new kitchen countertops. New floor covering and also paint can do marvels, therefore could opening spaces between spaces. Each residence will present you with an entirely various situation of opportunities, as well as it's up to you to establish which ones will certainly bring one of the most return when you offer or rent out the home.

Who Else Will Like your house?

Elders may be your main target, but they aren't the only buyers out there. Will our home attract various other age groups-- young couples or families with children?

You've currently tried to find an area near neighborhood solutions, yet tossing a good institution area right into the mix will certainly offer you much more options when it's time to offer or rent.

Making an Offer.

You've found a house and intend to make a deal. You've already spoken with a lender, and you know you could get a loan just before you offer your house you stay in.

Give Yourself Some Time

That brief situation was a fast-forward variation of just a few of the actions you'll take when you look for your very first property. You could be searching for something entirely different, something that fits in with the needs of the customers and also occupants in your town. You could not also make an offer on a residential property at the end of your search.

Don't be in way too much of a rush to purchase. Certain, it's exciting and you intend to discover that first home now, but are you truly ready? Can you make a deal as well as work out a contract without letting your feelings take control of? The more time you invest learning about your real-estate market, the much less likely you are to make rash choices about any one home.

There are numerous points you can do to make absolutely certain you are ready to get your initial property:

Devote time each week to study.

That consists of searching properties online, talking with neighborhood real-estate professionals, making trips to your court to inspect the rates of just recently sold properties, and then driving by those properties to assist you evaluate the going rates in certain neighborhoods.

Do some even more reading.

This book will get you started, yet you might think about getting more information regarding specific locations of the real-estate market. There are numerous publications and Web sites committed to specific aspects of the business. Acquiring your hands on this info might imply the distinction between failure and also success.Consider taking a real-estate representative licensing program. You'll obtain a fast intro to the legislations as well as custom-mades that impact your state as well as neighborhood area. Taking the training course does not mean you need to come to be a representative. Actually, that can work against you. Brokers should disclose their status to all possible vendors, and also some homeowner you approach will emphatically refuse to deal with a real-estate broker.

End up being associated with your neighborhood.

Join clubs and associations. Start creating a network of people which understand you are interested in getting property. Make sure your family and friends understand to call you initially when they find out about a property that sounds like a bargain.

Learn about home repair as well as construction.

Take a course at a neighborhood area university or go to weekend lessons at home enhancement facilities. You'll marvel exactly how promptly you can discover how to manage minor repair services as well as remodeling jobs. You could never learn how to build a residence, but you will find out a lot more about constructing parts-- enough to assist you approximate repair works and also identify a trouble when you see it.

Discover landscaping fundamentals.

Suppress allure is a top priority when it's time to sell or rent out, and you could conserve a large amount of money by managing landscape design chores on your own. A perfectly landscaped whole lot could sell a house, however it's an element that many sellers do not also think about improving.

Hang around driving around the area, getting to know the neighborhoods as totally as possible. If you see a home with a "For Sale" sign, call to get the details about it, including the rate. Printed materials are a great source, yet they hardly ever tell you where a property is located, and also when you're not accustomed to an area, you can not associate place to cost anyway. Spending time in neighborhoods will help you get a far better feel for the differences in costs based on place, and also you might simply find a spot that you're particular would certainly be the best option if the ideal residence starts the marketplace.

Constantly watch for investment opportunities.

In 2013 you could not have paid way too much focus when your buddy told you concerning a household that needed to sell their house rapidly in order to go on to a much better task. This year, you'll jump on that declaration and also compile sufficient information to look into the property.

Real estate doesn't need to rule your life, however brand-new investors generally agree that it does control it for a while. Once you're past the fundamentals, you'll find yourself unwinding a bit much more. The specifics will certainly come a lot more normally, and you won't worry over every choice you make. Take it slow down, keep your feelings in check, and also you'll discover success in the realty market

Chapter 2:
EMPHASIE ON YOUR GOALS

At this point it s just practical to tell you that I develop goals for virtually every little thing. I m a medical unbiased setter, and also I don t merely developed targets, I track as well as check their advancement, changing my activities as needed to achieve them. Okay, call it a health and wellness issues, however there are even worse addictions, al though my other half possibly would have problem developing just what those are exactly.

Having really goals has in fact served me well in life. I m living evidence that you could accomplish anything you desire to accomplish if you absolutely want it awfully enough and also established targets to achieve it. I am operating to attain my targets financially, in business, directly, and also with my relative. When I attack any kind of sort of one objective, I create an added during that area of my life and also proceed go ing.

This pattern has in fact made my life interesting. When I set out to learn Tae Kwon Do it really wanted baseball and after I attained all I desired in running my goal was to make a black belt. It was simple and, given, very optimistic, because I had in fact never ever done any sort of sort of fighting styles be-fore. Twelve years later on, I was a third degree black belt and also a world champ. That s the power of objectives, determination, in addition to having a course. Clearly, none of it would certainly have been possible without first having the objective.

Today, while I have gold medals on the wall area in my office, the most vital badges are the experiences as well as the self-confidence that could possibly come just via achievement. Beginning your very own company property investment company could very well be your Tae Kwon Do. It could be that factor that, once you acquire associated with it as well as start accom plishing, will certainly just receive your self-confidence in addition to your ability to do even more.

There are 2 sort of individuals in this globe: those who fantasize and also those who act. The difference in between them is big. This chapter will aid you narrow your desires to guarantee that acting will not be so complex. What keeps back a number of daydreamers is that acting on those desires shows up overwhelming, complex, and also puzzling. So in this chapter, not merely will certainly we function to develop your authentic es tate targets, nevertheless you ll start to see simply how the remainder of the 9 weeks is really an action strategy to attaining them.

A CLEAR PICTURE OF REALITY.

Jack Welch, the previous CEO of General Electric and perfect marketing business author, has an axiom: Face fact as it is, not as it was or as you desire it to be." He s definitely ideal. Encountering reality as it is permits you to take a look at the source of where you are. To me, this is among among one of the most important concepts in guide thinking about that once you acquire quality within your targets, you will have clearness on the most effective means to proceed.

Dan Sullivan, founder of The Strategic Coach along with my individual teacher for above a years, claims modification be gins by telling the truth, and you will have to do that on your own and also those around you. Developing targets couldn't hap pen alone. Think about the whole exercise as a group occasion. Consult your companion, your partner, or friend. Acquire a feeling of truth in terms of your funds. If you re damaged, investing is going to be difficult. Take a great, sincere check out the origin problems that have in fact obtained you to this location. Is it a profession that is going no location? Is it a failure to do the many points you plan to do in life? Is it investing behaviors that go out command? The more sincere you relate to the beginning problems the actual reasons for where you are in your life, the far better you can strike in addition to remedy those issues.

My little gal could aid me make clear the point. Someday, her valued iPod was swiped. So, being an outstanding papa, I obtained her an additional one. Within a couple of weeks, that people was taken, also. Now without an iPod and no chance of her daddy getting her one more one (I m not crazy), she bor rowed her brother or sister s iPod. When he desired it back, she snapped. Her temper was to her sibling for repossessing his iPod, nonetheless the authentic trouble is that she maintains get ting her iPod stolen. As soon as she deals with the source trouble taking a great deal far better therapy of her points she ll prepare to have another iPod.

This form of brutal sincerity isn t simple for children to hear. It isn t very easy for grownups to approve, either. As you assess your personal setting goal, be honest with on your own as well as identify the origin trouble for where you are in your life, in addition to do the job of repairing it. It will definitely make your goals a lot more legit, rewarding, as well as accessible.

WHAT DOES A REAL ESTATE GOAL LOOK LIKE?

A goal should be produced, particular, possible, and also have a target date. I have friends which are continuously trying to assault the home runs from the park. They claim they would like to possess an airplane, so they go after every long odds deal in a hopeless effort to put together the money to accomplish their rising objective. I don t view them as wise sponsors; I see them as individuals which play the lotto, wanting to acquire and also victory large.

Industrial real estate investing is a fantastic company if you have a lasting horizon. There are no routes to success. I desire there were. Really, long life in a busi ness helps you gain wisdom, as well as when you do that, you have actually gotten the unfair perk and also points obtain enjoyable. You start to be able to view the future.

Let me inform you how I uncovered as well as bought our residence I m living in now. Despite the fact that this is a domestic property tale in a business real estate investing publication, it works as a good example of acknowledging exactly what you really want and also pursuing it. Moreover, this is particularly the very same process I use to establish targets in my commercial real estate investing company, in my personal life, as well as in my family life.

By the time my partner as well as I had our fourth children, we recognized we would certainly require a bigger property. I had really done the spirit looking asked for to acknowledge precisely just what I wanted in life and in cluded my spouse while doing so. We really wanted a place to enhance our young people, as well as a location where we might spend time with them. Due to the fact that I really felt driving to and from job was a considerable wild-goose chase, I comprehended I desired a house within a two-mile span of my work environment. So the first factor I did was draw North, South, East, and also West limits on a map. That set up the basic area. Next off came our house itself. It needed to have at the very least 4 rooms due to our children. I wished to have a yard hill sight taking into consideration that the property investor in me understands that homes with sights treasure faster compared to residences without. Ultimately, I desired at the minimum an acre house with a substantial backyard be trigger in Phoenix they are unusual as well as, once more, it would help our house treasure in worth quicker over the long-term. I had a target price range where I really felt a home like the one I was hunting for would realistically set you back. There were different other levels we wanted our home to have, like a certain variety of washrooms as well as outside features, yet these were the have to haves.

In shorts, I truly desired a home that we might possibly delight in living in, however that I identified was set up to worth in time. I recognized that this would be a huge monetary assets, as well as I planned to do it right. I wasn't about to endanger the thankfulness in addition to long lasting worth to obtain the attributes I wanted for convenience. That would have been an emotional decision, as well as to me realty could possibly not as well as should not be an emotional purchase.

After looking into every house in my geographical range that satisfied my particular criteria, I discovered merely thirteen suits, in addition to none of them were readily available available for sale. Sounds like a difficult scenario, right? Never ever. It simply suggested I should introduce right into task. That meant speaking with each property- proprietor.

My first contact took the type of a specific note to each of the home owner telling them that I desired to elevate my kids in this neighborhood which we would absolutely be living right here a long period of time. I notified each residence proprietor I wished to purchase his/her house then directly hand provided each note with among my young people in tow. These folks got on. We talked record, that we were from the location, and that my companion grew in this area along with gone to the schools close by. All which was true. After talking with each homeowner and also offered an area of time, 3 of them became interested. After a couple of months one would like to market. The bidding procedure was in between us as well as a various other household along with to be truthful, we acquired your home since the resident really felt one of the most comfortable with us. She understood we d take great care of her home, elevate our youngsters as well as maintain the neighborhood up.Today, we still remain in this residential property, as well as it has more than boosted in well worth. Contrast that with precisely the amount of individuals investment homes. They have an unknown principle of merely exactly what they want, they lose sizable quantities of time driving about, acquiring flyers, having a look at residences that rarely evaluate up, calling property agents, and ultimately deciding on one that is the closest they could locate to simply what they truly assume they desired.

The letter, while certainly considerable in the future in the 9- week program, is the least fundamental part of the story right here. The most essential component is exactly just how I knew specifically just what I actually wanted with such surety that I was able to go to such lengths with such dedication to move a resident which was dismissing advertising and marketing to really market her residence. That s the driving lesson that I ve brought throughout all my real estate investing and also in every little thing I do in life. Pin point goal-setting is a found behaviors. You could do it, also.

YOUR PERSONAL FINANCIAL FREEDOM PLAN: FOCUS, NARROW, DEFINE.

For me, personal personal goal setting as well as preparing has really continuously pertained to focusing, narrowing, and also specifying precisely just what I desire, then recognizing that a person point with such complete accuracy and also such a dazzling picture that there is no doubt. Doing that takes asking on your own standard concerns concerning that you are, simply what you can put up with, precisely how com mitted you are, how long you're all set to wait, as well as merely what you re visiting endanger.

Self-awareness is the method, as well as I get clearness by beginning with completion in thoughts. What do you desire your life to be like now? 5 years from now? One Decade from now?

This is all essential. The most suitable picture when it involves home goal-setting is a ten-year target. See ing the future out that much will certainly aid identify your now and also your 5 years from now image. As soon as you have a pointer of specifically just what your 10 years from now picture appears like, you could view if the sacrifices you ll need to make from to day ahead are appropriate to you.

When I go through this workout along with I go through this regularly my target is continuously to acquire financial absolutely free dom. Financial flexibility indicated something different when I was solitary, something different once I got married, and something numerous with every kid we had. It s con stantly changing, and I am frequently altering. That s the method life is. Expect your goals to change, nonetheless just thinking about that they do doesn t mean they aren t worth having now.

Financial liberty to me cracks right into costs, total properties, as well as easy earnings. Easy profits is cash money that I do not need to work for as well as concerns me through my investments. Definitely, the net worth in addition to passive in come quantities that made up my initial objective as well as the ones that compose my objective today were along with are truly spe cific. I furthermore have a guaranteed routine I am working against. Really, a huge part of my motivation for setting the monetary freedom objective wasn t relating to money. It pertained to time. I want to have much more of it for my children as they got in school. I meant to trainer Little League as well as see my youngsters sporting occasions as well as plays. I additionally intended to have the moment to seek my own personal passions like running along with fighting styles and also, today, backpacking. Specific, I recognized it would certainly take years to obtain to the element where I would absolutely be that absolutely cost-free. It did. The compromise was that I would certainly not be around significantly when the children were youngsters. Was it hard? Yes, however not as difficult as it would be now to miss my eleven-year-old child s football computer game, or to not coach Little League All Stars.

I decided to do whatever I had to do when my youngsters were younger to ensure I existed as they obtained a lot much more active. My other half was on board maintaining that. It goes back to the pain of self-control versus the discomfort of remorse. It s difficult to self-control yourself to operate lengthy hrs, evenings, along with week-ends for many years at a time, skipping out on schedule with friends and family. The soreness of that type of self-control is actual when it s occurring. When it s over, the discomfort is short lived. Absolutely it s a memory of hard work, yet it s hardly awkward. Actually, the accomplishment feels fantastic and also has actually contributed to which I have actually become. The soreness of regret, on the different other hand, isn't really instant. It comes tomorrow, following week, complying with year, or fifteen years later on, and when it s right here there s no going back. It s hard to calm. That s the soreness of regret, and it can last the rest of your life.

My economic versatility objective continues to be to alter, and also I continue to be to do the many points I must to obtain it. The remarkable element is that although I am still actively working, I ve well established my life approximately be there for my youngsters, to travel the world, to seek enthusiasms like Tae Kwon Do as well as backpacking. Intending high has an approach of doing that. It takes you additionally, quicker. My time is required to me, and I have the cost-free dom to plan around my calendar as opposed to others schedules. My technique is working. I put on t share this per sonal tale to boast or to permit on that I am any better than any kind of individual else. I m notifying it considering that success isn t merely for the lucky or the blessed. It s for everyone regular people like me included as soon as you acknowledge just what you want.

Developing your specific target will certainly take some self-analysis. Below is a device and some examples that will certainly assist you as you seek to find simply exactly what you really want out of life from a monetary viewpoint. Just by doing that could you establish a home monetary investment target, an essential step to helping you accomplish it.

MY FINANCIAL FREEDOM PLAN.

Your financial Freedom strategy supplies instructions, objective, and context tor your residential property monetary assets. It offers the why behind the what and also helps you Focus your objectives.

My Vision:.

This is a clear emotional photo of your economically independent future.

Objectives:.

These are quantifiable objectives for winding up being a real estate investor.

My Strategies:.

This is a particular strategy to achieving the objectives.

Created right into Your Financial Freedom Plan

Statement:

Until now in this chapter, I have actually mentioned my objective, vi sion, worths, targets, techniques, as well as approaches. We ve talked about various of the outcomes. Here are a number of examples of Financial Freedom Plan statements to obtain you believeing:.

"By 2019, I want to be monetarily free by having 550,000 a month in easy profits.

My vision is to become a residential property financier so I can travel a whole lot a lot more, have even more time to invest with my family, and within 5 years create at least Sioo, ooo each year in very easy income, with possessions that are raising to cash my retired life.".

I desire to diversify my financial investments and also get an average return of 75 percent annually to make certain that I can achieve my retired life objective of S3 million by year-end 2020.

You could possibly discover these convenient as you produce your very own goals. Note merely how certain and vivid they are. The even more certain you can be, the far better you ll be able to take air conditioning tion in addition to understand when you have in fact arrived.

Don t fear if you might t complete this enter one rest ting. I suggest getting as much details as you might devote to paper on the initial explore, then allow it rest. Have a look at it daily and also customize as you function your method via your week. You ll find many triggers during your day that will certainly help bring quality to just what you really desire from life. And also bear in mind, just as a result of the fact that you make up all this down doesn t indicate it gained t modification as time pass es. It absolutely will. Consider this as an image, a benchmark, from which to begin.

YOUR REAL ESTATE GOAL: THE FOUR PARAMETERS

Simply, having a bigger vision, a vision of financial totally free dom, is important. It keeps you influenced throughout those difficult times and offers the job you do significance. You ll call for more than merely a vision of financial versatility to make it a truth. Success indicates obtaining really spe cific. It suggests focusing on a smaller sized action: your very first financial investment in a business residential property.

Similarly as you will certainly be collaborating with a

wider monetary cost-free dom strategy, you ll desire to start collaborating with your commer cial real estate financial investment objectives. Right here's the most convenient means of establishing those objectives merely limit your choices making use of the adhering to four parameters:

Product Type: Choose in between office, retail, multi-family, as well as a host of others in business real estate industry. In the following chapter, we describe the benefits and drawbacks of each.

Location: We talked a lot worrying this currently. This is just one of the most important requirements considering that area is the largest indicator of a home s future performance.

Cash: How much money will you have to invest or invested in a property offer? Be functional and also keep in mind, it shouldn t be your first financial investment buck.

Assets Structure: Do you want to go solo or generate some investor companions? The option is your own.

The kind that follows will definitely aid you arrange your ideas.

MY FIRST COMMERCIAL REAL ESTATE FINANCIAL INVESTMENT COAL

Take advantage of the 4 specifications listed below to identify specifically the sort of financial investment possibility you are interested in. The even more specific you can be, the far better.

The product kind I want to possess is:

Narrow to the kind of house you assume you want to

own.

My chosen area is:

Figure out in what part of area you prefer your house.

The cash I should invest is:.

Identify the quantity of cash you want to buy this venture.

My favored financial investment structure is:

Figure out whether you desire investors or companions.

Put together into your goal affirmation:

Right here are a couple of occasions of Commercial Real Estate Investment Goals: I have $12,000 to buy my first office structure in Phoenix, Arizona by December 31, 20XX.

I have $3,000 to buy an additional investor s residential property offer to learn the treatment. After I do this,/ will certainly wind up being a managing companion in a company real estate deal by March 31, 20XX.

I will pay back all my bank card debt by June i, 20XX, as well as while doing this wind up being an expen in one specific mar ket certain specific niche mini-storage in the airpon submarket in planning for my very first property monetary investment in 20XX.

To now, I still think of the 4 requirements to limit my following assets job, and also for me, the place criterion is one of one of the most essential. This is a basic yet helpful tool. You ll situate residential property is less concerning finding something that could possibly make you cash, and also a whole lot even more regarding limiting the choices up till you reach the best one that can make you cash money. There s a large difference.

Locating the ideal financial investment has a component of probability and also suggests that there is just one right invest ment. Narrowing down the choices up till you locate the most reliable one puts you accountable, shows that there are good deals of good possibilities available, as well as readies you when a fantastic opportunity comes your method. I recognize there are great deals of possibilities.

STRESS YOUR GOALS RIGHT NOW.

There's no time at all like the present, so make use of the kinds in this chapter or produce your very own utilizing the ones in this publication as a summary. Bear in mind all that discuss activity? It s time to take some today.

Position your plan and also your goal right into one note pad or maintain them in a different folder on your computer system. The key is maintaining everything together and also dated so you might live specifically what you ve written. Make your life strategy and also your business real estate spending target something you commit to on paper, so they are solid as well as authentic. Be as detailed as you can be so there's passion as well as life there. Evaluating a dazzling target will certainly aid you get through the problems. We do truly acquire what we consider, yet we similarly should act on just what we consider. Jotting down your method as well as your objective is an important very first air conditioner.

Chapter 3:
Where You Can Invest?

Residential Properties

Real-estate financiers could pick from a sizable selection of houses. If you favor to buy house prop erties, listed below's a review of a few of the different types of real estate readily available to you. It consists of suggestions that aid you recognize the types of houses you are looking at. In addition, details are supplied to help you understand just how the land that residences are boosted generally dictates the kind of buildings that are created there and also just exactly how they can be made use of.

(a) Single-Family Homes

A single-family home is established to suit one each youngster or group of people living together. There's often one major entryway as well as merely one address for the house it's the sort of property countless people think about when we listen to the term community. Single-family homes lack a doubt one of one of the most common kind of house real estate, along with they are the preferred option amongst most of individuals purchasing a house.

The land below a single-family home is almost

consistently part of the financial investment set, nonetheless some homes are improved rented great deals. You are probably to encounter residences on rented land in resort areas, where land is costly and also challenging to find, within church-owned improvements, along with in assisted-care facilities.Not all single-family homes are produced in the same way. They can be arranged right into numerous various groups,. and it is vital for real-estate investors to comprehend the differences in between them just before they get or supply.

The Site-Built House.

Site-built homes are the frameworks the majority of us are famil iar with. All of the components needed to build a home are delivered to the site, and after that a specialist places your home with each other item by item. Community building regulations dic tate merely exactly how the site-built house should certainly be built. Residence in a storm zone may be required to have heavy-duty wall surfaces as well as structures. Timber roof shingles roofing systems are in some cases forbidden in areas that lean to wildfires.

Building laws are made to assist residence builders stop safety and security as well as security dangers along with ensure that every house is a steady struc ture for the location it is in. The home contractor has to get each mits to finish your house, and as structure advances, neighborhood assessors arrive to confirm that the work being done complies with all constructing policies. The proprietor normally cannot move right into your home till a qualification of tenancy (Carbon Monoxide) is offered.

Made Housing.

Manufactured residential properties were previously called mobile residences or trailers. They are integrated a manufacturing plant to follow the U.S. government's Manufactured Home Construction and Safety Standards Code, acknowledged merely as the HUD code. Each made house or area of a home is identified with a red tag that guarantees the home complies with the HUD code.

ALERT!

Various lenders will not fund produced real estate much less your house is on a permanent structure not loosen up just on its wheels. Regularly check out framework disorder before continuing with a financing application. Made houses are built on a permanent steel body as well as carried to the structure web site on their own wheels. Usually the wheels are eliminated, yet often they're still visible under your home after it is finished. There ought to be a details plate inside the house specifying its day of manufacture. The plate is generally on or near the main electric panel, in a cooking area wardrobe, or in a bed room outfit. The data plate is necessary considering that it offers details regarding your house's initial air conditioning and home heating systems, plus different other devices as well as components. The information plate similarly educates you the wind zone and snow great deals for which the home was developed.

Made real estate is in some cases harder to re sell. New home bundles that do not need a down payment are so appealing that purchasers commonly team to them before purchasing a resale. Study the location where you are buying to discover previous sales of pre-existing manufactured houses.

Buyers normally get manufactured property as part of a land-home package deal that's created by the shops that offer the residences. Rates of interest are often above the rates provided for site-built home financial investments, but the strategies project because of the fact that purchasers can normally relocate to a home without a down payment.

Made real estate acquires approved for FHA and VA fundings. Some areas in addition to housing developments will definitely not allow manufactured real estate. Specific acts often fool tain constraints versus created real estate, additionally if there are comparable residences on great deals surrounding the parcel. It's crucial to make sure any kind of type of home will definitely be al lowed on the land you mean to put it on, so inspect all connected constraints just before you buy a made residence.

Modular Homes.

Customers are usually perplexed pertaining to the differences between modular houses in addition to manufactured homes. Modular houses are partly integrateded a manufacturing facility, yet that's where their resemblance to made real estate ends. Modular houses are established to conform to certain building regulations at their place. Then the sectors are trans ported to the house website on flatbed trucks, where they are positioned on a prebuilt structure, signed up with, as well as finished by an area contractor.

Modular residences have in fact altered significantly in the last few years. Initially, many of the modular residences supplied by makers were straightforward one-story cattle ranch homes that appeared like a doublewide produced property. They were easy to find when you were home acquiring. Now the designs are endless, and also unless you already existing to see a residential property provided and also put together, you would most likely never think it's a modular. Makers could conveniently attract methods to please your specifications or make changes to tailor among their already existing layouts.

Lenders typically fund modular homes in similarly they money site-built houses. An evaluator might or may not talk about that a house is modular on an ap praisal. Modulars are generally appropriate in devel opments where site-built houses are the norm. Analyze limiting agreements and also action constraints to be certain you can develop a modular home on the whole lot you would like to obtain.

Are modular residences marked to assist determine them?

Yes. Look inside the kitchen location cabinets and also bathroom vanities for a typed page that's glued to an upright panel. It offers the modular business that developed our house along with specifics worrying the aspects utilized within it. Modulars can commonly be created much quicker compared with an internet site-established home. Their parts are created inside your residence without environment delays, and the production facility element itself assists price manufacturing. The expenditure of a modular residence is usually much less each square foot compared to for a comparable site-built home, making them interesting purchasers, yet rate can vary quite a bit by maker and design.

(b) Multifamily Dwellings.

Homes, townhouses, duplexes, fourplexes each of those structures are taken into consideration multifamily residences, different homes that are housed within the identical framework or team of structures. Some multifamily systems are deeded in various means compared to single-family residences. The titles for houses, townhouses, and also cooperatives are regularly de scribed as being a hybrid sort of ownership. That's be induce the residential properties include aspects of real estate that are had by folks as well as elements that are had by a group of folks.

Condominiums, or Condos.

An individual which has a condominium has the drawback do system simply, not the land underneath it. That shows houses can be piled on leading of each different other. Some condo minium developments have actually frequently been owner- populated, yet you'll possibly experience former apart ment complexes that have actually been converted to condos.

All apartment proprietors in a development share possession of common areas, such as the land, the outside of develop ings, passages, roofs, swimming pools any type of area utilized by all proprietors. A homeowner' association generally cares for the condo development, collecting costs from owners in order to preserve the common places. Condo proprietors pay real estate tax simply on their certain gadgets. The association pays property taxes on the common areas.

Condominiums situated in visitor places typically have a home management business on the properties, making it easier for proprietors to lease their units. The agents in those workplaces might give you a smart suggestion of rental poten tial and also the expenses associated with working with the business to market along with rent out the residential property. You could work as your own property manager, but utilizing a firm that is presently developed to market rentals could bring greater returns, also af ter the cost of spending for their solutions.

ALERT!

Some condo and also townhouse limiting covenants do not allow you to utilize your device as a rental. Discover the plans associated with each home prior to you make a deal to purchase it.

Townhouses, or Town Homes

Townhouses are commonly a series of solitary or multistory systems that are urled each other flat by com mon wall areas. Townhouse proprietors have their systems as well as the land below them, so townhouses could not be piled on top of each other. Owners of townhouses pay property taxes on their certain gadgets and also the land under them.

Typical areas are had collectively by all townhouse extremely owners, as well as they are handled similarly as condominium minium developments are.

Exactly how Do Cooperatives Fit In?

Cooperatives, additionally called co-ops, generally resemble apart ment buildings or condominiums. All house that's element of a cooperative is had by a firm. Customers obtain stock in the firm as well as are shareholders not proprietors of property. Each investor has a lease to his device that runs for the life of the firm. New participating financiers need to normally be accepted by an administration board.

Real estate tax are paid by the company, and also home mortgage are usually held and paid by the company. Costs to run the residence are shared by all share owners. Cooperative ownership is not usual in a great deal of states.

Duplexes and also Fourplexes

Some individuals make their first real-estate financial investment a du plex or fourplex, a structure which includes two or 4 homes. These structures can look like a condominium or townhouse development yet with less devices. It isn't truly unusual for the framework as well as the land it hinges on to be had by somebody, nonetheless it is feasible for the systems to be separately possessed.

This sort of residence could be an excellent way to get started with economic assets. Several proprietors stay in one system in addition to lease the others, allowing the occupants' rental cost pay the home loan as well as assisting the owner build equity in the property.

(c) Dealing with a Residential Development

Rather than acquiring already existing properties, you might decide to get a system of land and create it into an area for one or more of the real estate selections we merely dis cussed. Going from bare land to a residential subdivision takes a huge amount of research as well as readying. There are roads to create, utilities to generate, constraints to put in place to make sure a steady neighborhood, and great deals of various other considerations you have to make just before you could possibly move on with the work.

Accessibility of Utilities

To build a domestic complex, you'll need access to electrical power, phone, water, and sewer system systems. Just how far will you need to run electric and also telephone lines to obtain to the residential property? Exactly how will those tasks affect your advancement deals? Are water as well as sewage system links easily available to the forecasted good deals? If not, will you produce a community sys tem for each and every energy, or will property owner be respon sible for placing unique wells and septic tanks?

Is the land proper for certain septic tanks, and if it is, just how much must each system be from a well or various other wa ter source to avoid contamination? A septic sys tem functions such as this. Fluid waste from washrooms, the kitchen location, cleaning, as well as various other areas is reached a big storage tank. The waste starts to break down in the container in addition to become a sludge-like liquid. When it reaches a drainpipe on top of the container, the fluid blood circulations right into pipelines that extend right into a network of gravel-lined trenches, called a drainpipe field. Gaps along the length of the pipelines introduce the fluid into the trenches. The fluid seeps right into the dirt below the drain industry, where microbes along with oxy generation in the filth complete the neutralization procedure.

Land loadeded with rocks or clay-like dust does not drain eas ily, so larger drain locations as well as great deals will be required. The minimal dimension of the whole lot relies on the sort of systems made use of in your area, the legislations that regulate the positioning of those systems, as well as the topography of the land. A detailed soil analysis must be leadings on your to do list for this type of housing development.

A layout study could be had to assure your development makes ideally use of the land. A questionnaire needs to be done to validate the development's limits, in addition to each great deal must be checked individually in order to divide it off from the larger system. Your neighborhood legislations will definitely manage many of the jobs you need to execute prior to setting up the land.

Roadway Work

Another vital activity is building roads to access the great deals, as well as it's probably that rules will certainly control the minimum road width and exactly how roads are produced. If you need to cross an extra person's land to acquire to your development, a lot more laws will certainly lend a hand to cover the right- of-way that's asked for to allow long-lasting and lawful air conditioning cess.

Is It Worth It?

You'll have funds invested in the land and the enhancements. The amount of good deals can you really acquire from the system? Simply just how much are comparable lots setting you back in your area, and also precisely just what's their common time on the market? Do the math to figure out if you can recuperate your expenses as well as earn a revenue.

If You Work with Builders

Many individuals that develop land for lesson never ever create a house themselves. They want to stick to lot sales as well as let the brand-new proprietors develop their very own homes. However, occasionally it's simpler to market a new home on a large amount than it is to supply a whole lot that's unoccupied. Talk with area service providers to see if any kind of among them have a passion in dealing with you to establish spec homes speculation houses that are developed to market to the general public in contrast to for a particular individual. Evaluate each service provider's references, along with get legal understanding just before starting a spec residence task.

Smaller sized Developments

Smaller sized advancements could be based on fewer ideas. Speak with your community preparing board to determine if a tract of land can be separated right into 2 or 3 parcels without needing you to adhere to stiff subdivision fast overview lines. If so, you could be able to market bigger whole lots to consumers which desire to have more land for individual privacy or different other aspects, while bypassing the official permissions that are required for class advancement.

REALITY

Although class specifications are firm, it's a smart idea to follow them as thoroughly as practical even if you commonly aren't compelled to. The regulations were executed for a rea youngster, along with remaining within the guidelines can make your land a whole lot more appealing to future customers.

(d) Limiting Covenants

Restricting agreements are deed limitations that place on house situated within a particular advancement. Restrictions provide the advancement a more basic appearance taking into consideration that they handle the kinds of homes created there and a few of the activities that occur within its expected areas. Restrictions are usually written by a lawyer that helps the developer and that uses the designer's objectives for the house to compose the phrasing.

When they are implemented, restraints help secure property values. They almost always define the very little dimension of homes enabled within the advancement, how many residences could be improved one lot, and also just exactly what sort of construction your houses need to or need to not be.

The adhering to topics are generally set out in limiting commitments:

- Drawbacks precisely how much frameworks need to be from roads and good deal lines
- Easements as well as rights-of-way, such as a path for high-voltage line or future road development
- Assessments owners need to spend for roadway maintenance or other costs
- Information that information just how limitations could be changed or nullified
- Guidelines concerning animals as well as various other pets
- Guidelines that control at home companies in addition to house rentals
- Regulations that control tree-cutting, fencing, along with various other landscape layout issues

Together with those common plans, you might view clauses that try to minimize mess on whole lots, or attempt to develop a sense of harmony by identifying merely exactly what colors you could possibly repaint a home or which products are forbidden for usage in construction of new residences.

Restricting commitments have absolutely nothing to do with zoning or government laws. Those are both different issues versus that you should certainly discover prior to making a deal on a residential property.If you find a property that you want to place an immediate deal on, yet you have not yet assess the restrictive agreements, put a data backup in the offer that states you could possibly back out of the agreement without penalties after evaluating the constraints. Area an affordable amount of time on your endorsement.

In many cases brought in restrictions are taped on activities. Read the vendor's act to confirm there are no additional limits that will definitely disrupt your planned use of the home.

(e) Easements as well as Rights-of-Way

An easement is the right to utilize an additional person's land for a specific feature. It could be written to make certain that it puts on a home generally or to a certain part of the land. Easements can cover any type of issue on which both events concur, as well as they often end up being a permanent part of the substitute both parcels. A right of way is an unique sort of easement that provides an individual the right to travel throughout home had by another individual.

An easement does not have to be offered a person. It might be written to profit a property rather. For examination ple, Mr. Smith provides present and future proprietors of a bordering tract the right to cross his the home of access a close-by lake. The surrounding landowner could be made it possible for to create a street or simply utilize an existing roadway. One more sort of easement may permit the bordering resident to place an exclusive well on Mr. Smith's home, with irreversible water lines triggering the close-by parcel.

An irreversible easement can furthermore profit a firm or a company. An utility business can deserve to set up power lines or conceal energy lines on a system of land. A housing innovation can be offered an easement that allows it to build along with solution a water storage fixate another person's residential property.

Easements could similarly benefit a person. Mr. Smith might permit a certain individual to cross his the home of a/c cess the lake without connecting the authorization to a system. This sort of easement generally expires at a spe cific time or occasion or after the fatality of the person which obtains from it. These easements are not normally contributed to an act description.

Possible Problems

Easements could have an adverse impact on house values. The landowner which gives the easement usually might not construct structures within the easement place or usage fence that would hinder access to the easement owner.

ALERT!

Before you purchase any sort of type of home, you should understand where each one of the easements exist in addition to specifically simply how they restrict your use of the land. Understanding the specifics concerning easements is necessary for any kind of land you purchase, whether it's family, business, or commercial. An additional downside of easements is buyer understanding. Potential purchasers are typically turned off by the reality that others have any type of sort of right to make use of the land. If the easement is for something like high-tension high-voltage line, the negative sensations are stronger. Not only are those lines unpleasant, many individuals consider them to be a health danger.

Just since an easement is not being utilized doesn't imply

it will definitely never ever be taken advantage of. If an easement is a permanent part of your act, there's continually a chance that the person which capitalizes on it will certainly choose to take advantage of it. Talk with a knowledgeable real-estate legal representative to learn exactly what activities you might need to do away with an extra easement from your act.

(f) Boundary Surveys

A boundary survey exposes you particularly where a parcel's home lines exist. The survey ought to be each developed by a proficient, accredited surveyor. The lines involving the home are marked with a mix of iron pins, concrete post, or other irreversible items. By referring to spots such as rocks in addition to big trees, the land surveyor furthermore cuts a training course along the line, which is specifically valuable for picturing residential property lines in timbered places

REALITY

Typically the land surveyor's programs, called cut-throughs, show up for years after a survey has actually been performed. Visibility depends on the topography at property lines and also whether the proprietor has tried to keep the path lacking weeds as well as other plant.

In some areas, studies are a routine incident when ever before home is marketed, however in different other areas, the purchaser must choose whether a research is required. It's consistently a plus to get a research study, likewise if your financing carrier does not need it. Don't be lulled into thinking that alreadying alreadying existing fences mark the property lines. If the fence is aged, the here and now proprietor can not know who constructed it and whether it adapts house limits. Various sellers do not know the loca tion of their limit lines whatsoever.

Make your deal to assets depending upon your authorization of the resulting boundary lines. If there are concerns, such as a close-by framework that extends into the land you are acquiring, you want to uncover them be fore you buy. The vendor must responsible for clear ing up any sort of kind of concerns that influence your use of the house as a result of improperly significant boundaries.

Exemptions to the Rule

Implementing a survey never wounds, yet occasionally you may determine it isn't truly necessary. If you're acquiring a currently existing ing residence in a development, in addition to there are research studies on get that advancement, you could likely use them to find previous questionnaire marks. The distance in between each marker must be videotaped on the study, so you could obtain an exceptional suggestion whether the real markers are positioned where they should be.

In some areas, it's typical for a supplier to spend for a study. In others, it's considereded a buyer expenditure, yet that doesn't indicate you cannot ask the vendor to spend for it. The seller could decline pay the whole deal, nonetheless you could be able to bargain a bargain to split the expenditure. Furthermore, research studies that have been done in existing years can generally be upgraded for a lower charge compared with a brand- brand-new survey. If you're investing for the questionnaire, find which performed it last in addition to ask concern pertaining to an update. Al means have your research study videotaped at the area court home or an equivalent location that houses public documents. You would absolutely be stunned at exactly just how generally research duplicates are lost by owners. If the land surveyor passes away or goings of company, you could not have access to a replicate unless it's part of the general public documents.

Industrial and also Industrial Properties

Teaming up with company or industrial houses provides an entire brand-new array of chances for real-estate investors. Industrial houses consist of apartment createings, shopping center, coin laundries, as well as limitless different other kinds of real estate built to suit companies and also services. Below is a sneak peek of numerous of the kind of properties you could experience if you choose to get commercial real estate.

(a) Apartment house

If you're a people-person, having as well as dealing with an apartment building could be the excellent economic investment for you. It can be a huge complex or a building with just a number of systems. One thing's undeniably handling a selection of renters recommends you'll never have a dull day, and also you'll have a lot of chances to exercise your settlement along with diplomacy capacities.

Are leasings secure in your area? The rental market varies, nonetheless recognizing simply exactly how it has really accomplished in the remaining couple of years will certainly assist you identify if an apartment building stands out financial assets choice. Simply exactly what are occupants searching for? Visit ads as well as check out the rental market really carefully that can help you determine which characteristics are in most of demand, afterwards set out to locate a residence that matches the specifications, either as-is or with updates.

How Much Is It Worth?

If you find a structure of interest, you'll should develop the quantity of it's worth. Positioning a value on an apartment building is a various process compared to you run into when you get residential property. Its worth is linked very closely to the rental revenue it generates. If you choose to purchase it, you'll at some point have the building evaluated, yet a fast methods to sneak peek its worth is to make use of the gross earnings multi plier approach, or GM for short. The GM is a number that's identified by examining the normal sale price that equivalent apartment building have actually set you back versus the amount of rents they make.

Can I establish worth using the average asking prices of homes that are currently for sale?

The rates that vendors put on homes are often inflated enough to make it possible for a minimum of a little bit of agreement location, considering that buyers like to feel they are obtaining a bar gain. It's even more precise to make use of actual list prices to assist you establish value, since they stand for reality costs that buyers wanted to invest for similar properties. Let's consider a circumstance. Think about a structure with 5 residences, each making $600 each month in lease, for a total amount of $3,000 normal month-to-month incomes from the entire framework. The building recently cost $324,000. Right here's merely how you would definitely compute its GM:

1. Multiply the total normal month-to-month lease by the number of months in the year to find the annual gross earnings: $3,000 x 12 = $36,000.

2. Split the price the building cost by its yearly gross earnings to obtain the GM: $324,000/$36,000 =9.

Now think of that the building you mean to get is actually just like the structure utilized in the example, except that its full yearly rental fee is a bit lessened, at $30,000. Change the formula around and also rise the GM by the building. Total yearly earnings to approximate its worth $30,000 (INCOME) x 9 (GM) = $270,000 (ESTIMATED VALUE).

Calculate the GM for as bunches of apartment-building sales as you could locate to assist you set up an understanding of the typical GM for that sort of home in your location. A real-estate representative which is proactively entailed with advertisement sales can give you information about offered homes as well as give a viewpoint of the typical GM.

Increase Rental Income to Increase Property Value.

Does the building have untapped capacity? Updates may allow you to raise rental fees, causing a rise in earnings and home value. Do the math, as well as find out the amount of it will establish you back to make the modifications. Can you af ford to do the work? The amount of can you boost rents with out reviewing the ordinary rental costs in your place? For how long will it call for to recuperate the expense of the renovations at the brand-new rental cost levels, presuming complete tenancy? If occupancy decreases, so will certainly your capital. Can you proceed the task without harm to your financial resources?

If being a home manager isn't really in your plans, it does not show you can not acquire apartment buildings, as long as you don't mind handling renters for a short time. You may acquire an apartment building, make improvements, elevate rents as well as worth, and after that resell the property to a various other financier. Find out how long it has really taken similar houses to supply, and also identify whether you might truly rent the home at boosted expenses prior to you choose to do.

Evaluate the Seller's Documentation.

When you get an apartment house or any sort of structure with rental renters you need to ask to view duplicates of all current leases or rental setups. It is not unreasonable to ask the seller to expose you previous income-tax re turns as well as down payment slides to verify that the leasings have in fact produced the amount of profits that is being asserted. Most of vendors are straightforward, however enables confess: It isn't really hard to offer a possible purchaser inflated profits figures in the hopes that verification will not be requested. You should furthermore evaluate energy costs for the previous couple of years if the structure proprietor accountables for paying them. If the seller is handling a real-estate agent, the broker more than likely has copies of the files you require.

At closing, all lessee down payment have to be transferred to you from the former proprietor. Make sure that top ic is addressed in your deal to get any sort of kind of home in which security deposits are held by the present proprietor. Research the leases to discover their terms and also to find when they finish. It's ideal if they do not all end at the same time, particularly if you plan to replace your homes as well as raise leas. Your whole owner base could abandon at once, hobbling your capital till brand-new occupants are located. Connect with a real-estate legal representative if you generally aren't rather specific ways to analyze the regards to the leases.

(b) **Workplace Buildings.**

Office is typically leased for a certain buck quantity per square foot of space, with rates varying generally throughout the nation as well as within the exact same community. Rates change with the financial situation and with supply and also need the much more available location, the much less rental fee you can request for. Given that job along with rent rates can be emergency clinic ratic, office structures are not usually the best alternative for a starting investor which does not have reserves of cash money to entice from throughout down times.

Like different other company structures, the worth of an office building is linked to the quantity accumulated from its leasings. You can take advantage of the GM method explained on page 29 to determine an approximate worth for a building. Spend some time to study the office rental circumstance in the neighborhood where you intend to spend. Exists a requirement that hasn't been filled out? Possibly there's a demand for little suites, however a lot of the space presently offered is for larger busi nesses. Can you locate a framework where collections could quickly be made?

Receive

Keep updated with the demands of neighborhood companies by establishing a network of calls within the business area. The team at your neighborhood chamber of commerce can probably offer you a list of clubs and other teams comprised of regional businessmen, sign up with a couple of-- their members are excellent get in touches with. Go to common council conferences. Being familiar with the folks at your local planning board. Speak to business real-estate agents, those who offer and those which handle commercial residential properties, to learn exactly what their leasing as well as customer business owners are looking for. If one type of property maintains popping up on most- wanted lists, get imaginative-- attempt to determine if you could offer it by making changes to an already existing residential property.

TRUTH

If your downtown location is on the edge of renewal, you may be able to find structures that can do double obligation, with retail stores on the ground level and also workplaces or household apartments upstairs. That method is usually used in tiny to mid-size communities and cities.

Buyer Beware

The ideal scenario is to locate something in an excellent place that, with some work, can be turned into a building that's more eye-catching to occupants. Your improvements will be overseen by building examiners, and also you must figure out whether prepared modifications will comply with neighborhood zoning ordinances as well as disabled accessibility laws. Constantly protect yourself by inserting backups in your deal to acquire that give you time to discover your strategies just before you make the final dedication to close on a property. If you could not make the adjustments that will certainly place a structure to its best usage, there's no reason to buy it.

Numerous rental arrangements for office space make use of a web lease, a lease in which tenants pay for a portion of the structure maintenance. You will likely receive leases from the previous owner, so be sure that your acquisition agreement consists of a condition that provides you the right to research those leases just before you acquire the property-- as well as to back out if you don't like what you see. Similar to various other rental structures, all security deposits ought to be transferred to you at closing.

(c) Retail Buildings

There are consistently lots of types of retail properties offered for financiers to buy. Exactly what's a retail residential property? Think benefit and also purchasing-- any type of structure that houses a business where everyone goes to buy a product. Regular kinds of retail properties include huge as well as small shopping malls and also other structures occupied by pizza shops, restaurants, clothes stores, convenience stores, supermarket, drug stores-- it's a countless listing.

ALERT!

Check neighborhood policies to find out the regulations that apply to handicap vehicle parking for any sort of type of business building you prepare to buy or restore. Ensure the parking area is huge sufficient to include room for handicapped as well as various other consumers.

Finding a good location for a retail building is somewhat different from finding a great area to situate a workplace or other advertisement property that the public usages in some way. If you're shopping for a set of footwears, you expect to be able to obtain to the building conveniently and also to park in a convenient as well as safe place. If you can't, you'll go to a various other shoe shop.

When you see your physician's workplace, you 'd such as those functions, yet you will not necessarily transform doctors merely to obtain them. Comparing the locations you like to shop with the areas you stay clear of is a really personal way to begin reviewing retail places.

Stores can exist on any kind of level of a structure, however rooms found on the structure's entry level consistently regulate more rent, even if an elevator is offered to take shoppers upstairs. Excellent vehicle parking is vital, as well as sometimes congested parking lot can be remodelled to give more rooms and also a much better circulation of web traffic.

Leases for Retail Buildings

Relying on their location, retail structures could be rented or leased by the square foot or by the amount of frontage they supply along a busy road. Frontage is identified by measuring the overall linear feet the building occupies along the length of its major entrance-- the side of the building that's probably to entice consumers. That method is usually made use of for preferred places in hectic buying districts, where retail room is in much demand. The square footage technique is a choice that can be used for any kind of residential property.

Some property owners need retail tenants to authorize a portion lease, where a portion of the lease is based upon the tenant's gross or earnings. The lease usually includes a minimal quantity of lease that's due regardless of what the occupant's income. You'll locate that leases varya fair bit from area to location, so you have to do some research to learn which kinds are regular where you live.

Investing in Strip Malls

Huge mall run out the reach of a lot of financiers, however small strip malls are usually cost effective.

You've seen them-- they're retail complexes where companies are usually housed side by side in one long building, although L-shaped malls as well as various other setups are additionally typical. For ideally client web traffic, a shopping center ought to consist of at the very least one store that appeals to a vast sector of the population, such as a clothes merchant, a food store, or a chain drug store that stocks various other products in addition to pharmaceuticals. Extra lessees that can complete the spaces are pizza shops and also restaurants, florists, health-food establishments, as well as numerous other kinds of boutique.

Having a great mix of businesses aids the shopping center attract lots of people, and that allure drives traffic to the complex, profiting every company in it. Exactly what's a great mix? That combination varies for every single area. As an example, if there's a college nearby, a great mix may be companies that appeal to university student and also various other individuals. Exactly how around a bookstore, a duplicate store, and perhaps an establishment that focuses on delivering bundles?

If your strategy develops a constant circulation of clients, it will not take wish for renters to see favorable outcomes, and also flourishing tenants implies continued capital for your residential property.

Take some time to research your local market. Which shopping center in your community appear to constantly be rented out? Have the exact same tenants inhabited those centers for quite a while, or does there seem to be a steady turnover? Why do you think individuals are attracted to the preferred malls? The more understanding you have right into a shopping mall's success, the most likely you are to make your very own venture an effective encounter.

(d) Industrial Possibilities

Industrial residential properties are an unique sort of commercial realty. Industrial websites are not often places where you would go to purchase a product or discover a solution. They are often the locations where products are made or distributed.

Tiny and large manufacturing plants and also distribution centers for retail or wholesale items are all examples of commercial properties. Industrial residential properties differ, yet they have a single thing alike-- most need a lot of investment funds as well as knowledge from their owners. They are most ideal stayed clear of up until you feel certain you can deal with a big task.

Industrial buildings that have actually been made use of to make an item can be strained by ecological issues that should be dealt with prior to you purchase. This is particularly true if you plan to convert the residential property to ensure that it's ideal for a various market compared to it presently offers. What was made there, and also did the location around the building deal with the dumping of any kind of waste?

Zoning rules are essential, as well as you have to work properly with planning boards and various other companies on the regional, state, and also federal government degrees. Move slowly and also very carefully.

Don't deal with any type of sort of commercial job up until you acquire lots of experience, or even then look for added insight from specialists in the field.

REALITY

Having a tiny industrial park that includes simply the distribution end of a number of firms is one means to get in the area of industrial property. Find out if mail-order firms or various other types of storage facilities are seeking room in your area. A location that's close to a flight terminal and also prominent delivery agency places is constantly a plus, as well as access ought to permit access as well as exit of large trucks.

(e) Land Development

Developing a piece of raw land in an industrial location can be complicated or simple, depending on the task you prepare to embark on. In some areas, development is regulated on a neighborhood degree; in others, the state is much more entailed. Your certain job could possibly also be subject to government laws. Whatever you prepare to do with the land, make certain your strategies adapt all applicable laws and regulations.

Prior to you make final prepare for the residential property, you should look into zoning and ecological concerns in order to find out if there are constraints ashore usage. Even if zoning isn't a problem, deed limitations may avoid you from making use of the land for certain objectives. An action can mention that the property cannot be utilized for industrial functions. An action may even protect against a particular sort of business from being built on the land. As an example, the previous owner might likewise own a neighboring lawn-and-garden facility. Just before offering the land, he inserts a clause stating that the land cannot be made use of to operate a lawn-and- yard business. It's constantly important to examine a property's deed that can help figure out just how the land can be made use of. Concerns about ecological problems, such as the presence of secured wetlands, are another vital concern that ought to be solved prior to you acquire a tract of land.

ALERT!

Exist plans for brand-new roads or widening already existing roadways in your location? Those enhancements are frequently a signal that city governments are anticipating growth in the location. It's beneficial to research the reasons behind the roadway renovations as well as consider land near places where improvements are planned.

Land Speculation

You may prefer to leave the land alone, holding on to it and marketing for a revenue when its market value has enhanced. That type of financier is called a speculator-- a person which gambles that a tract will rise in value at time in the future. Whereas some are merely hypothesizing that the value will certainly climb based upon basic styles, others have inside expertise regarding a forthcoming task that will certainly make the land better. The risk of being a land speculator is that land worth may drop rather than up, as well as you'll have to hang on to the property till it comes back up once again.

Do your homework if you decide to buy great deals and also land for eventual resale. Ensure there's an energetic market for the sort of property you intend to acquire. You may be betting that the area you buy will grow over the lasting, which is fine-- just as long as you are readied to rest on the home until that happens.

In some cases a lot that will not offer as primitive land is easy to relocate if a house is on it. Talk to builders concerning the possibility of setting up a spec residence-- a house improved speculation and also marketed to the general public. Seek advice from a knowledgeable real-estate attorney before authorizing an agreement with a home builder.

Great Option for Beginners

Investing in untaught land is within the reach of beginning investors, yet you'll need skilled guidance to lead you through the many regulations as well as policies associated with land development Large land tracts can be good assets if you are quite acquainted with the area and have an excellent feel for just what the land may be helpful for now or in the future. You could hold the investment up until the per-acre market value reaches a level where it makes good sense to offer, or you could move forward with some type of development.

Lots for Manufactured Housing

One development alternative is to build whole lots for manufactured housing, which may be rented to people which have manufactured homes. Inspect neighborhood regulations very carefully prior to you start an advancement for produced real estate. If you can locate the right land, with energies that are readily offered, this kind of development can be a rewarding financial investment.

Recreational Vehicle Parks

A RV camping area can be a fundamental center that deals with tourists who require an area to stop for a solitary night, or it can be a full-service park with a swimming pool, miniature golf, and other feature you 'd such as to bring in. The majority of Recreational Vehicle parks supply concrete pads and utility connections. They can be situated along a significant freeway or in a traveler destination. Study already existing Recreational Vehicle campgrounds to discover the common services as well as costs that tourists run into in various areas.

Self-Storage Centers

Most of us have way too much stuff. That's most likely one factor that self-storage facilities are so prominent. Steel buildings built on concrete pieces are one of the most common setup for these prominent systems, and unless you wish to offer climate-controlled locations, the structures you lease don't even need to be heated or amazed.

Collecting rental fees from renters can be a migraine, as well as some tenants that stop paying may never obtain their goods. It isn't uncommon for storage centers to public auction items left by occupants in order to cover past-due storage costs. Secure on your own with occupant down payments and a good rental arrangement, as well as select a terrific location to see exceptional returns from a storage facility assets.

(f) Finding Expert Advice

This chapter has actually touched on only the basic information about purchasing industrial properties. As you end up being more associated with real estate, you'll experience several sorts of residential properties and also a limitless number of concepts for prospective assets. Despite which is you opt to pursue, do your research and also consistently obtain professional insight just before progressing with a deal.

Below are a few of individuals you could contact for recommendations concerning commercial residential properties:

- Commercial real-estate brokers could help you discover similar homes in order to establish worth and could keep you notified of new lists on the market.
- Personnel at your neighborhood planning board as well as various other comparable companies are essential get in touches with for info regarding land development, zoning, and also several other concerns
- Team at your county courthouse could reveal you the best ways to watch tax maps of land and locate public details concerning the existing proprietor's mailing address.
- Surveyors and also evaluators give services that can be important to your success. Learn more about the professionals in your location so that when you have a concern, you could get it responded to.

- Lawyers who specialize in real-estate purchases can help you prepare a deal to buy industrial homes and also follow up with lease contracts for your occupants.
- A tax specialist can supply essential advice that can help you framework you assets.

Industrial homes can be profitable, however they are riskier and require more funds compared to purchasing a solitary household home you mean to rent or re-sell. You can be successful if you look into the marketplace, recognize the laws associated with the type of property you have an interest in pursuing, and also relocate very carefully to get it.

Old House Renovation Pros and Cons

There is something hauntingly magnetic in a century- plus aged, neglected property. It rests on its site like a stray young puppy, looking at you with mournful window-eyes, sprouting plants and also drooping shutters, whispering, "Imagine how terrific I could be if you fixed me up." You can visualize on your own in a shaking chair on that wrap-around porch drinking lemonade in a future fixed-up variation. Can your dream match fact?

Before you sign on the dotted line, you might want to look at exactly what it will certainly require to get to that fully-renovated- rocking-chair scene. Utilize the following pros and cons to figure out whether you are a good prospect for having an old home.

Pro: Neglected aged residences can be contended rock-bottom deals.

Few residents want to do just what it takes to repair an ancient house. Preferably, you ought to have some house repair/improvement experience to defray prices, however as a whole, sprucing up an aged house has great assets capacity.

Disadvantage: Sometimes acquiring an old home that needs refurbishing is equivalent to the price of buying a brand-new home.That is not consistently real, however unless you look very closely at the house and also calculate the cost of repair works with a big margin for mistake, you could be in for a shock. Obtain a comprehensive home inspection just before you accept purchase. The largest restoration costs will certainly be replacing a structure, roof, plumbing system, electric system, and also setting up HVAC where there was none prior to. Make a decision whether you would rather purchase a brand new house over an old one which has been remodelled for regarding the exact same cash.

Pro: Old houses were built to last a long, very long time. Construction techniques and also engineering may have come a.long way, yet that does not imply brand-new houses are better. Since home builders frequently take the less costly course, or have way too much on their plates to guarantee quality construction, residents of brand-new houses can find themselves with a shoddy framework looking for significant repair services. At the very least with an aged home you know exactly what you are in for: the fundamental foundation, as well as some sprucing up.

Con: Nothing lasts forever.An older house may have

endured the examination of time, however you could securely assume something is crumbling. Your first major interested in any sort of house, old or brand-new, should be the foundation. Take a marble and also drop it in each area of the initial floor of our home. Does it roll as if it is on a hillside? Pay attention to how the floor really feels in various parts of each room. If the floor really feels spongy, bouncy, or makes something else in the space jiggle when you bounce, the foundation has problems. That doesn't indicate you must abandon that particular residence, but be ready to invest a lot of money for an architectural engineer, heavy devices to jack your house up, as well as a new structure. A qualified residence assessor should have the ability to tell you the amount of job will need doing, both for the foundation and also other significant issues.

Pro: An aged property has actually character.Even to the individual with no education in style or style, the difference between a contemporary "box" residence and an older house is screamingly noticeable. Wood is anywhere, often with detailed specific. The lights vary from luxuriant to lovely. Even the equipment (light buttons, doorknobs, hand-made nails) has personality.

Con: Character is rarely square.Whether you plan to work with a woodworker for maintenance and repairs or do the job yourself, just quit on the suggestion of anything going like clockwork. You have to employ a lot of imagination and trial and error, as well as sometimes you will certainly have to have some features customized."Character" could also be translated as drafty and noisy (aged residences creak and moan a great deal). Sometimes you could fix, recover, or change, however frequently you will certainly merely discover how to live with the adverse side of "character." If you intend to market, bear in mind that numerous possible purchasers could not love the much more eccentric features of your old house.

Pro: Any products that lasted this long were high quality.

Old houses were usually built with heart ache, cut from the facility of old trees so fatty tissue with resin that they normally push back bug as well as water damages, seemingly permanently. Craftsmen as well as home builders made use of actual materials; there were no faster ways, exteriors, or affordable alternatives. Central warmth as well as air were non-existent, so designers usually incorporated passive solar and also ventilation design to capitalize on air flow and also hinder mold.

Con: Old property products are sometimes hazardous, and also costly to get rid of.

Two noteworthy examples are lead paint and asbestos, both of which bring possible carcinogen, either during elimination by taking a breath the dust, or if some young adult in your house chooses to communicate with them (picture a kid gumming the windowsill).

Pro: You can pay for more square footage with an aged property.

Several of those aged residences are substantial. You can obtain lost in the square video footage, going sideways or vertical. And also the ceilings heights maintain smaller rooms from feeling boxed in.

Disadvantage: The mortgage is economical, however the energy costs are through the roof!Chilly drafts, lofty ceilings, a big, rambling home - it's a dish for a problem each time you get the mail.Updating an aged home to be power effective is complicated, especially if you own a historic house with local compensation needs to do nothing to the house that would certainly jeopardize its historical stability, such as changing leaded glass windows with power effective vinyl ones.

Pro: An aged house that you become your home will certainly be uniquely yours.

It will not be a cookie cutter residence, appearing like the one next door, nor will it be dull. Nobody else will have one like it, and also it will certainly become a part of your family members.

Disadvantage: Becoming connected to an old house can bring heartache if you need to offer it up.

Economic economic crisis, job transfer, as well as far better schools are all factors that family members move from one residence to one more. When your heart, perspiration and blood are poured into a residence, it can truly hurt to give it up.

Are you still crazy with that said overlooked aged home? Then go all out. A love for aged homes is the most vital requirement to having one and revealing its previous glory. Aged residence remodelling is unforeseeable, yet it will certainly enhance your life.

How to Use Land When Investing In Real Estate Investment

Perhaps you have consistently imagined transferring to the nation, as well as getting "back to the land." Yet what will you finish with? You could mow hundreds of acres throughout the growing season, and also have a pristinely-manicured landscape around your country home. That would certainly be enjoyable. Or, you can make a prepare for your land to return a little on your financial investment. Take into consideration these concepts.

Conservation

Whether you have woodland, a pond, a verdant meadow, or a swamp, you can grow your land especially for the perk of wild animals as well as indigenous plant varieties. This plan needs an interest for the atmosphere as well as a selfless wish to put your powers right into preservation, due to the fact that it will not make you rich. Devoting your land to preservation will possibly turn the cash-flow outward. Yet if you desire an environmental hobby as well as have the cash to fund it, this is a worthy and also gratifying plan that will reap perks - although some of the advantages you or others might not completely comprehend for awhile. However that's the beauty of doing something excellent on principle. In the meantime you can bask in the simple beauty that nature will repay for your hard work.

Tip: Contact your state's preservation company. For

example, the Missouri Department of Conservation releases an annual plant order form for native trees, shrubs and also plants. Bundles of types are cost preservation, wild animals cover, and wildlife food (crazy berries, seeds and also nuts).

Make Hay

You do not need to be a farmer to allow your land fruit and vegetables. Do you have a verdant field? You could have the ability to avoid summer cutting if you allow it increase for hay. If you reside in a farming neighborhood you might also have the ability to let someone else (with their very own tools) do the job. This is called sharecropping, however don't consider it in the blog post- civil battle sense, and don't use that word in the classifieds. Rather, ask for someone to "bale hay on halves." This implies you will offer half of the harvested hay bales to the interested party in return for trimming and baling. A 10 acre pasture could easily create over 20 huge round bundles in a season.

Organic Farming

If you are a skilled green thumb, elevating unique organic crops can be a hobby, or fulfill your wish to feed healthy and balanced meals to your family. With organic fruit and vegetables increasingly popular, natural farming may help your household's earnings. Success would certainly depend significantly on the type of dirt and the physical characteristics of your land, as well as how much time, effort as well as cash you are able to spend. Chemical-free farming is maybe among one of the most work intensive methods to utilize your land, yet it can be rewarding.

Animals

Maybe you will not make money with a cattle ranch on ten acres, however if you've consistently intended to maintain a couple of cows or equines, you can. Or you could raise llamas, Nigerian Dwarf, goats, or Border Collies. In theory, you could keep more pets of a tiny breed on 10 acres compared to you might beef cattle, but the number you maintain per acre will certainly rely on the kind of land (timbers, arid scrubland, etc.), whether you turn pastures for eating, and several other factors. You could make a little farm financially rewarding with these endeavors, but be ready for vet costs and intensive study to obtain one of the most out of your stock.

Birds

Have you ever imagined on your own increasing early every morning to scatter grain for your barnlot group - Rhode Is land Reds, Pekin ducks, Guinea fowl as well as turkey, with a couple of geese sprinkled in for watchdogs - and also collecting fresh eggs for your breakfast plus a few dozen to market to passersby that react to your homemade "fresh eggs" indicator by the roadway? While that picture is a little glamorized, increasing chickens as well as various other fowl supply many advantages: fresh, organic eggs as well as meat (thinking you can stomach slicing off heads), less pests in your backyard as well as garden if you keep free-range fowl, and maybe a little of pocket change.

Bees

Assuming you do not have serious honey bee sting allergies, maintaining hives on your home can be a reasonably passive form of added earnings, particularly if you start by permitting beekeepers to position a couple of hives on your home while you find out the procedure, as well as possibly obtain some honey as "rental fee". Or you may intend to keep honey bees to pollinate your nectar-bearing trees, shrubs as well as plants. Get started by calling a neighborhood beekeeping club or online forum. Beesource.com is a handy location to start.

Trees

Your return on investment will certainly have to wait years longer for a farm including tree crops, whether they are fruit, nut, wood or Christmas trees, but you could earn a little bit a lot more once they grow. Xmas trees can be particularly rewarding, relying on your location, direct-marketing tactics as well as determination to handle everyone.

Berries

Strawberries, raspberries, blackberries, blueberries - all these fruits are high-end produce at the marketplace, and well worth your time, even if you expand them only for your very own enjoyment. Growing berries for sale is work demanding and also could require hiring temporary help during har-vest. You-pick berry farms are an alternative, however prepare to manage various other issues like liability insurance coverage, marketing, and also obviously, dealing straight with clients.

Winery

Ten acres for a vineyard- It's a start for a wine fanatic that might develop from a hobby right into a rewarding and also effective enterprise. Just like any sort of small ranch company start-up, you should intensively investigate the subject as well as look genuinely at the amount of assets funding you have to start with. A winery calls for a little bit much more in facility costs, for instance, compared to other plants

Bed & Breakfast.

Couple any of the above suggestions with a charming estate, an ideal area, as well as a love for hosting guests in your house, and also you have the dish for a gratifying occupation. If you don't live in a cutesy village, you could attract visitors with the little plant or herd you elevate on your land. Some B&B facilities permit visitors to putter in the garden, harvest organic crops, interact with the animals, or just delight in the rural view as they soak in the Jacuzzi.

Using ten acres is never a simple matter. It's ideal to begin tiny, think about your family members's requirements as well as desires, and devote a lot of time to research study. One of the most satisfying way to utilize your small story of land is to grow, increase or plant something you will take pleasure in for several years

Chapter 4:
Dealing with Real-Estate Agents.

There will certainly be times when you make use of a real-estate broker that can help you buy and sell investment homes. The method is finding the very best broker and also comprehending just how the agent's commitments impact your purchases. Discover your local laws and personalized, then placed that expertise to work that can help you locate a real-estate agent that will certainly offer you a phone call whenever a residential property that suits your demands starts the marketplace.

Exactly how Can an Agent Help?

Successful real-estate brokers monitor their regional markets every day. That's crucial, because various other investors are on the lookout for properties as well as Home buyers are always hunting for a bargain. The most preferable residential properties merely don't remaining. By developing a relationship with several brokers, you will certainly be among the very first to read about brand-new opportunities.

Should Real-Estate Investors Become Agents?

Real-estate brokers are generally needed to reveal that they are licensed brokers an instant turn-off for some "available by proprietor" vendors, often called FS- BOs. Agents have to additionally follow certain marketing tips as well as various other state and also federal laws. Hold off un-til you're sure a certificate will certainly help. Working with a real-estate representative streamlines a few of your study. A lot of agents have access to a neighborhood multiple listing customer service (MLS), an empire of firms that have actually made a decision to group to reveal and also market each other emergency room's listings.

Brokers could look into properties marketed via the MLS as conveniently as they could watch current listings. Recognizing the sales past of properties is a real plus considering that it enables you to find out exactly just how much each home cost without having to dig with neighborhood public records.

Working with an agent who actually viewed those marketed residential properties can help you make even better contrasts, since the broker will certainly have individual understanding of each home's disorder at the time of sale.

REALITY.

A representative might describe MLS printouts of sold homes as comps, or comparables. They look precisely like the MLS sheets for current listings, yet they likewise include the listing and also sale date, the sales amount, the name of the selling agent, and also in some cases also the sort of financing made use of. Comps aid you make comparisons to identify an existing list's market price.

Acquiring Listed Properties.

Using a broker is the only method to gain access to properties noted with a real-estate firm, so it's best to plan for that beforehand by finding a good agent now. Don't let the representative ignore you-- make periodic call even if you work primarily with FSBO properties.

Offering and Leasing Properties.

You may determine that you wish to use a company to sell as well as rent your very own properties, particularly if you own property that's located a long distance from house. Hiring a company is a great choice when you do not have the moment or experience for efficient advertising and marketing or if you have an one-of-a-kind residential property that could be handled better by a specialized professional.

Working with a Seller's Agent.

A seller's representative is any type of representative helping the real-estate firm utilized by the vendor to offer a residential property. In an MLS.

setup, all offices work to sell each other's lists, so even if Firm XYZ holds the actual agreement, all real- estate representatives that can show the property are probably subagents for the seller. Considering that agents work for the seller, buyers ought to never divulge private infor- mation to them.

Vital Agent Disclosures.

Real-estate agents in the United States made use of to operate on a buyer-beware basis. Brokers worked to get the very best bargains for the seller, yet they did not reveal the representative- vendor connection to possible buyers, which often incorrectly assumed that the agent was working for them. Buyers often felt free to give the representatives confidential information-- such as just how much they were readied to spend for a property-- unaware that it was the agent's duty to pass that details on the vendor.

Nondisclosure caused countless suits and grievances to state real-estate licensing boards, so disclosure policies started to advance. Nearly all real-estate representatives in the United States are now required to reveal that they are agents for the vendor, and also in many cases the disclosure must be in composing.

This suggests a seller's broker may ask you to authorize a document that confirms she discussed real-estate agency standing with you. It is not a contract but just a statement that validates she described her association with the vendor and also the selections you have when you deal with a real-estate representative. The record is often come with by a hand-out that explains the different sorts of company relation-ships readily available in your state.

Disclosing Material Facts

Seller's representatives must make known worldly facts regarding a home. That includes things like dripping roofing systems and also structures, plumbing and drainage troubles, drain and also septic problems, broken home appliances-- anything that is wrong with the home.

Disclosure doesn't simply concentrate on maintenance and repair concerns. A restau-rant that's doing business in an area not zoned for that sort of company is a trouble that needs to be made known to potential customers. If a structure on the residential property touches the property line of a neighbor, the information have to be interacted.

Commonly divulged material facts differ from area to location. In California, representatives are asked to make known whether the residential property is on a fault line. In areas susceptible to flooding, the residential property's relationship to the flood plain is an essential disclosure.

Fact

Repossession may or could not be thought about a material fact. If no legal files have been filed, repossession does not often need to be divulged. If legal filings have actually occurred, repossession is normally considered a mate-rial truth.

There's likewise information that is exempt to disclo certain. A vendor's representative needs the vendor's authorization to disclose personal info regarding the seller. For in position, the broker will not inform you that the sellers are getting a divorce, can't stand to be near each other, as well as will certainly take any type of deal that comes! Learn as much about disclosure personalizeds in your location to make sure that you'll identify if a typically revealed product is missing as well as exactly what type of details you must not anticipate to get from the broker.

Dealing with a Buyer's Agent.

Numerous representatives will certainly supply to function as a buyer's broker, some-one that agrees to represent your interests. If you're in the market to acquire home and also like to work with a buyer's representative, the purchaser company contract you sign might re-quire that you function specifically with that person. Non exclusive arrangements are readily available, however most agents will certainly not work in that ability. Being a purchaser's representative takes a large amount of initiative, so representatives aren't inclined to devote time and energy to your search if you are not dedicated to stick with the connection.

If you authorize an agreement with a representative-- as either a purchaser or a seller-- you are the representative's business owner. If you authorize a disclosure for a seller's representative, you are a customer. The broker needs to act in an honest way and deal with a customer's deal with treatment, yet he owes much more loyalty to a client. Some states allow buyer's agents to function briefly with a verbal agreement, giving the agent and the customer the opportunity to get to know each other just before authorizing a formal contract. Typically, the verbal agreement has to be placed in creating just before an offer is made on a home. Never sign a contract with an agent until you make certain the representative is the best selection for your demands.

The Agent's Duties and Responsibilities

Buyer's brokers have added duties and responsibilities to the buyer that seller's representatives either aren't obligated to perform or could not execute. Primarily, a

customer's representative need to be loyal, maintaining the purchaser's each personal information personal. The buyer's representative should also disclose all known facts about the properties that are up for sale
and the sellers-- anything that could possibly influence the purchaser's decision to make an offer.

Customer's brokers also give aid by researching previous sales to assist create a proper deal for the property; recommend agreement backups to shield the buyer's passions; and are closely involved in the closing process. This includes helping the purchaser to discover a lending institution, tracking the development of the funding, purchasing assessments, collaborating with the closing officer-- every detail that will get the buyer's contract to the closing table.

Working out the Buyer Agency Agreement

The specifics of a customer company agreement can be worked out with the broker. Right here are specific levels you could tricksider including in the agreement:

Browse location: You can restrict the geographical location an agent works in, preventing broker overlap if you are hunting for homes in multiple areas.

Interval: Agreements can remain in force for any sort of length of time you both agree to, also as little as eventually or for the proving of one property.

Exceptions: You can ask the agent to insert an exclusion that enables you to collaborate with and also purchase FSBO lists on your own, without paying the representative a cost.

ALERT!

A real-estate company that calls itself an "special customer company" bargains only with customers and does not accept listing from sellers. That kind of company consistently functions to get the very best contracts for their buyer customers.

Buyer's representatives are typically paid a part of the vendor's compensation at closing. Ask your agent if any kind of situation alreadies existing under which you would certainly owe him a compensation. Don't authorize an agreement till you comprehend every term within it.

Working with a Dual Agent

Double company takes place when a purchaser's representative shows the buy emergency room a listing held by the agent's real-estate company. Twin agency is a little challenging because the broker has responsibilities to both celebrations. The representative can not disclose personal details to either business owner about the various other, but need to still beware to ensure the needs of both business owners are fulfilled.

Twin agency is typically simpler to take care of if the customer is not working with the agent which actually holds the listing for the property. Numerous real-estate offices are so accustomed to taking care of dual company that they encourage their agents not to babble about the individual business of their business owners. Then, when dual portrayal occurs, only the listing broker is privy to personal details.

Twin agency is not allowed in all states. Where it is

allowed, it should typically be disclosed to the purchaser and vendor beforehand, and also both have to agree to it in composing.

Various other Agency Arrangements

Your agent may clarify other types of firm guidelines, and these appear to regularly transform in order to comply with the demands of customers and vendors. Pay very close attention as representatives disclose working partnerships, and ask as several inquiries as essential to comprehend where their loyal associations are.

Below are some added terms you may listen to:

Solitary agent: A single broker could help either the customer or the vendor.

Designated representative: In some states, the broker accountable might designate a marked representative to a transaction, bypassing the dual-agency circumstance to permitmuch more full buyer as well as vendor portrayal.

Purchase broker: A transaction agent assists facilitate a closing yet does not have an agreement with either event. (This setup is lawful in Florida.).

Locating the Right Agent.

The very best agent for you relies on how you plan to use that broker. Even if you're in the market to get, a seller's agent might be the very best selection if you don't require recommendations and also want to handle the bulk of deals by yourself. You just require an agent to submit deals to sellers with detailed homes. There's no reason not to use a seller's representative if you feel comfortable proceeding by yourself, developing agreement backups and time frames and also identifying the most effective rate to supply for a home.

If you 'd like a little more assistance, a customer's representative could provide it. If you prepare to deal realty, you should locate a broker that excels in both areas.

Calling the broker on the "For Sale" indicator places you in contact with the seller's representative-- not somebody that's going that can help you acquire the very best rate on a home. That's penalty. You could not need any help-- just see to it you do not inform the representative anything you wouldn't desire the vendor to hear.

Start Looking.

If you know you'll utilize an agent periodically, you may want to start surfing the area to find one who clicks with your personality. It could take you some time to find somebody you depend on, so begin looking now. Below are a couple of tips to obtain you began:.

- Ask your close friends if they had an excellent experience working with particular brokers on selling and also buying properties.Pick up homes-for-sale magazines and pay attention to the lists as well as marketing techniques of individual agents and also companies.

- Surf the Internet to contrast regional real-estate agent Web websites or to locate a broker in one more location.Look for key phrases concerning your community on popular Internet online search engine to learn which agencies in your area ranking highest.

Meeting representatives. Pay attention to each representative's enthusiasm and knowledge of the real-estate market.View properties with an agent without signing a contract. Investing a few hrs with an agent will expose a large amount about her personality as well as motivations.Bear in mind of each agent's interest and also level of involvement. Did the broker follow up with you after the session to recommend various other properties?

Reality.

A brand-new representative can be just as effective as an experienced pro. They're enthusiastic, they require business, and given that they're collaborating with fewer clients, they typically provide outstanding customer support for each one.

There's no ideally means to discover a terrific broker-- it could take some time, or it could occur on your first try. Often you just need to go with your gut impulse to determine if a representative is the "right" one for you.

Collaborating with Multiple Agents.

Often purchasers think they will find much more homes by dealing with an individual at every firm in town. Whether that works or otherwise depends on your area,. however the business can backfire.

If you're searching in the city, where brokers in some cases work a very specific area, it may be best to create a partnership with greater than one broker. Even if they be lengthy to an MLS that covers a broader base, they could only tell you regarding homes specified in your area they wish to operate in. It can be a logistical problem for them to move past those limits, as well as they might not feel educated concerning residential properties located in various other areas. Ask each agent to define the locations where he works. The same is true in rural areas, where residential properties can be expanded over a multicounty area. The brokers probably understand about listings outside their base, but they might not be anxious to drive you hundreds of miles to discover them.

Merely ask, as well as they'll inform you where they could reasonably function.

Calling each one of the firms in town can really backfire in villages, where every agent recognizes each other as well as everybody draws from the same group of lists. You may be shocked just how quick word takes a trip regarding customers that call every agent requesting for specifics concerning the exact same residential properties. Call as numerous representatives as it takes to locate a good one, yet remember that if you call everyone all the time, you won't be taken as seriously as you may such as.

Acquiring the Most from Your Agents.

In the real-estate world, we spend a great deal of time talking about agent obligations-- just what brokers should and also shouldn't do to follow legislations and values. We don't listen to almost as much about customer as well as seller tasks, as well as they are every bit as crucial. Simply put, your real-estate trans activities will be a lot more effective and also less difficult if you treat your broker in the same way you want to be dealt with.

Get Your Finances in Order.

Speak with a lending institution to discover exactly what kinds of financing are readily available to you. Do not waste everybody's time looking at lists that are out of your cost wide range unless you feel a residential property can be bought for much less than its asking cost. If you're preapproved for a lending, you'll feel a lot more confident concerning making a deal, as well as your loan provider will certainly have offered you a close estimate of the amount of you can expect to pay in closing prices-- an essential factor to consider when you make a deal.

Be Clear and also Honest.

The sort of information you provide a real-estate broker depends on your partnership with the broker, but whatever the connection is, be truthful. If you're working with multiple vendor's representatives, let them understand to ensure that their efforts don't overlap. It's a waste of everyone's time and will ultimately produce hard sensations. You prepare to be in this game for a while, so let every person know you are straightforward and honest.

When you're buying or marketing any kind of special residential property, do a bit of study to find a representative with the competence to handle the deal. For instance, if you're buying or marketing business residential properties, a commercial broker is probably your best choice.

It also assists if you're able to communicate just what you want and needs. The best property could not be available. Do you want to wait for it, or do you intend to compromise as well as find something that you can modify with a little job? Determine which qualities are most important to you, and share the listing with your broker. A representative cannot develop something that does not already existing, yet the majority of them can do a respectable work of searching for properties with most of your must-haves

Cooperate with Your Agent

Don't thoughtlessly comply with a representative's regulations, but do try to cooperate. If contracts must be signed, do not let them hang around. Your offer could be disposed of if you wait as well lengthy to deliver files or assured down payment cash. A better offer could be presented at any moment-- can you guess whose anonymous agreement is void when that occurs? Do not refuse to enter a home simply considering that you don't like its outside. When you have an appointment, you should at least take a quick walk through the residential property. It's disrespectful to drive away, as well as it produces hard feelings among agents. It's in your benefits if your broker is on excellent terms with the various other brokers in town.

Do not assume you could properly evaluate a list by looking at an MLS sheet. Your agent has probably been to the residential property and recognizes that the image or description is terrible and also not a real representation of the property. Select some of the properties you would like to see, however trust your representative to choose some, also. You'll be amazed by the amount of residential properties that you would certainly have disposed of are in fact great finds.

Your representative will likely visit the home assessment, yet you ought to attend too, if possible, so that the examiner can reveal you problem areas as well as speak with you directly concerning them. Existing to ask the inspector questions provides you a far better feel for which repair service issues are important and also which are small. Some things sound much worse on paper than they really are. Becoming aware of them secondhand via your representative merely isn't really as insightful and requires the broker to explain something that might be out of his industry of expertise.

Remain on Top of Closing Issues

Take care of all concerns required for your lending. Choose your closing agent if that applies in your location. Collaborate with your broker to make sure everything is ready for closing, such as switching utilities and also obtaining insurance policy binders. Your representative will certainly aid, yet those products are your responsibility.

Real-estate closings do not simply occur. They happen be-cause at the very least one person is following through, normally on a daily basis. You'll find that the roadway to closing is a great deal smoother if everybody does his share of the job.

ALERT!

Do not expect your broker to do anything prohibited or anything including fraudulence or deceptiveness. Vendors shouldn't ask their representative that can help cover up an architectural trouble. Buyers should not expect their broker to write a deceitful co-system. Keep in mind that representatives should comply with reasonable housing issues; they could not guide a buyer to or far from specific areas

Chapter 5:
Real Estate Financing

Regardless of what some late evening infomercial may lead you to believe, the is no such point as "totally free" realty. Realty is a commodity and also must be paid for. As a real estate investor - one of the most essential roles you will play is to create your offers using a range of various funding tools. This chapter is visiting instruct you the ins and outs of different approaches you could use to money your real estate financial investments.

In This Chapter, You'll Learn About:.

- Why You Need to Understand Real Estate Financing.
- All Cash.
- Conventional Mortgages.
- Portfolio Lenders.
- FHA Loans.
- 203K Loans.
- Owner Financing.
- Hard Money.
- Private Money.
- Home Equity Loans as well as Lines of Credit.
- Partnerships.
- Commercial Loans.
- Other financial investment Tools.

Why You Need to Understand Real Estate Financing

The objective of this chapter is to fill you in on the many different types on property financing that you could make use of in your real estate investing. This chapter is made to help you transform those strategies right into truth. If you have any concerns regarding any of these real estate financing strategies, do not think twice to look the BiggerPockets internet site for more details.

Ultimately, the adhering to listing is never detailed, however will certainly offer you a good idea of some of the funding methods used by investor to finance their real estate. By having a great extensive overview7 of these approaches, you could incorporate an investment motor vehicle, a financial investment method, as well as a funding method to manage any kind of property financial investment.

All Cash

- Numerous financiers opt to pay all cash for an assets home. Based on a recent joint research bv BiggerPockets as well as Memphis Invest. 24 % of US investors use 100 % of their very own cash to fund their realty assets. To be clear: also when financiers use terms like "All Cash," the reality is no "cash" is in fact traded. In many cases, the buyer brings a check (often approved funds such as a mortgage lender cashier's check) to the title firm and also the title business will write a check to the vendor. Other times the cash is sent out through a cable transfer from the bank. This is the most convenient type of funding, as there are generally no difficulties, but for the majority of financiers (as well as most likely VAST majority of brand-new financiers) all cash money is not an alternative. Additionally, the return offered from an all cash money deal will certainly not be the same as when leveraged. Lets discover this additional via an example:

Real Life Example:

John has $100,000 to spend. He could opt to make use of that $100,000 to purchase a home that will generate $1,000 per month in revenue or $12,000 per year. This equates to a 12 % return-on-investment.

John can additionally, instead, use that $100,000 as a 20 % deposit on FIVE comparable homes, each listed at $100,000. With an $80,000 home mortgage on each, the cashflow would be approximately $300 each month per residence - which is $1,500 per month each or $18,000 annually. This relates to a 18 % return-on-investment - 50 % much better than purchasing just one residence.

Conventional Mortgage

As you could see from the instance above - funding your financial investment home could produce considerably better returns than paying all money. Most investors, rather, opt to finance their financial investments with a cash deposit and a standard typical home mortgage. Many typical conventional home loans call for a minimum of 20 % down, however may extend higher to 25-30 % for investment properties depending upon the lending institution. Conventional home loans are the most common sort of home loan utilized by home customers and normally offer the most affordable rate of interest. Go here to find interest rates in your location.

To get more information concerning mortgage funding as well as exactly what you can qualify for - look into the Bigger Pockets Mortgage Center.

Portfolio Lenders

Typical mortgage loans can originate from a range of sources such as financial institutions, home mortgage brokers, and also credit unions. In many cases - these borrowing sources are not really utilizing their very own resources to fund the lending however are acquiring or borrowing the funds from one more party, or marketing the loan to government-backed institutions like Fannie Mae as well as Freddie Mac in order to replenish their own funds. Consequently - most lending institutions should follow an extremely rigorous collection of regulations and also tips when it comes time to financing a financial investment. These strict rules could make conventional financing hard to acquire for numerous - especially genuine estate financiers as well as various other self utilized debtors.

Nonetheless - some banks as well as credit unions have the capability to lend from their very own funds totally, which makes them a profile loan provider. Since the money is their own, they have the ability to supply even more versatile lending terms as well as certifying standards. This implies that they are able to make lendings readily available at any sort of terms acceptable to them. Oftentimes a portfolio lending institution will certainly have funds available with much less limiting credentials compared to a typical loan provider.

Many financial institutions or lending institutions do not promote that they are a portfolio lender - but you could locate these individuals via recommendations and also networking with various other financiers. You could likewise simply get hold of a phonebook, call every one, and simply ask if they supply portfolio borrowing.

FHA LOANS

The Federal Housing Administration (FHA) is a United States federal government program that guarantees home loans for mortgage lenders. If you have medical insurance or vehicle insurance coverage you currently recognize the idea: merging cash to spread out the danger for everybody. FHA fundings are designed just for property owners which are visiting stay in the property - so you can not utilize an FHA-backed funding to purchase a pure financial investment home. Nonetheless - you can take advantage of the exemption to the regulation that permits the FHA-financed home to have up to four separate units. In other words - if you intend to stay in among the units, you might purchase a duplex, triplex, or four- plex.

The advantage of the FHA funding is the low-down repayment demand: presently simply 3.5 %. This can aid acquire you started much sooner, considering that you don't should save up 20 %. However - every true blessing possesses a curse. While the low deposits the FHA offers is excellent - the FHA does call for an additional repayment, called "Private Mortgage Insurance." This "PMI" insurance policy protects the lending institution and is needed when the down payment on an FHA financing is less than 20%. The additional PMI repayment could make your monthly repayment slightly greater, hence lowering your cashflow.

Property & Live Rent Free

A sub-set of the FHA financing, the 20 qK financing is a loan that permits a home owner to acquire a residence that is in need of some rehab job - and also gives them the ability to finance those repairs or enhancements into the lending itself. Like the regular FHA loan, the 203K funding still allows for the reduced deposit requirement permitted by the FHA (presently just 3.5 %.) This financing kind is also appropriate for duplexes, triplexes, and fourplexes, but maintains the same need for simply being for "owner occupants" as well as has Private Mortgage Insurance needs for fundings under 20 %.

203K Loans

Real life Example:

John discovered a small duplex for $100,000 that he wants to relocate into, with plans to stay in one half as well as lease the other half out. The home requires regarding $12,000 for brand-new paint and also carpet. John has the ability to consist of that $12,000 into the price of the financing and also pay simply a 3.5 % down payment on the overall quantity for a total of$3, Q20 down. John can now get the new paint and carpeting (spent for by the loan), relocate right into his remodelled house, rent the other half, and also start making cashflow and also building wealth. John is a happy camper.

Home Patli Mortgages

An additional Government Backed Loan- the home course Mortage was introduced by the Government had Mortgage Giant Fannie Mae in an attempt that can help turn their non-performing financings (homes they have confiscated on) right into rewarding fundings once again. Like the FHA loan, the Home Path program allows for smaller deposits (currently as reduced as 10 %) yet unlike the FHA - no home mortgage insurance policy is needed as well as the lending is offered for investors and also "non-owner occupied properties. The HomePath program likewise includes the capability to finance repair works into the acquisition like the 203K FHA funding we discussed previously. The catch, nevertheless, is that these financings are just offered on Bank Repos possessed by Fannie Mae. To hunt for houses readily available for the HomePath program, check out the HomePath website at HomePath.com.

Proprietor Financing

Financial institutions or various other gigantic loan provider are not the only bodies that could finance a property for you. Sometimes - the owner of the home you would like to buy, could actually fund the property, as well as you will just make your monthly payment to them rather than a financial institution. Commonly, the only time a homeowner will do this for you is if they already own the residence free-and-clear - implying the vendor can not have a current home loan on the property. If the seller does have one more lending, and after that sells the home of you - the vendor's funding have to be repaid quickly or deal with repossession. This is because of a lawful stipulation written right into nearly eveiy lending called the "Due on Sale" provision. This stipulation offers the previous loan provider the right to call the note instantly due. If that quantity cannot be paid - the loan provider has the right to confiscate on the residential property. Some financiers decide to ignore this condition and still acquire "based on" the other lending - risking that the financial institution won't foreclose.

If the problems correct, owner financing can be a

fantastic means to obtain possession of realty without utilizing a bank. Proprietor financing could likewise be a great device for selling your properties in the future as well, which we'll cover more in chapter eight when we check out "exit methods."

Hard Money

- Tough money" is funding that is acquired from personal business or person for the objective of investing in real estate. While terms and also styles alter frequently, Hard Money has a number of identifying characteristics:

- Loan is largely based on the value of the home.

- Shorter term lengths (due in 6-36 months.).

- Higher compared to regular passion (8-15 %.).

- High funding "points" (fees to obtain the funding.).

- Many difficult money lenders do not call for revenue confirmation.

- Many difficult money lenders don't need credit history references.

- Does not show on your individual credit rating record.

- Hard cash could often fund a deal in just days.

- Hard money lenders understand when the property needs rehab job.

- Hard money can be beneficial for short term fundings and also circumstances, however numerous investors that have used hard money lenders have been put in hard scenarios when the temporary lending ran out. Utilize difficult money with care, making certain you have several leave methods in position just before taking a tough money financing.

- To locate a difficult money lender, try the following pointers:.
- Ask a Real Estate Agent.
- Ask a House Flipper.
- Check out BiggerPockets' Hard Money List.
- Newspaper.
- Craigslist.
- Google It.
- Mortgage Broker.

Private Money

Exclusive money is similar to Hard Money in several aspects, yet is normally distinguishable as a result of the relationship between the lender and also the customer. Commonly with "exclusive cash," the loan provider is not an expert loan provider like a difficult money lender but rather an individual aiming to attain higher returns on their cash money. Often times there is a closer relationship with a private money lender ahead of time, and also is these lending institutions are commonly a lot less "business" oriented compared to hard money. Private money often has less charges as well as factors as well as term length can be worked out a lot more quickly to offer the most effective passion of both parties.

Exclusive lending institutions will certainly lend you cash to acquire residential property in exchange for a certain interest rate. Their investment is protected by a cosigned promissory note or home loan on the home meanings if you do not pay - they could seize as well as take the house (similar to a financial institution, difficult cash, or most other funding kinds). The interest rate provided an exclusive lender is normally developed up front and also the cash is provided for a specified time frame, anywhere from 6 months to thirty years.

An exclusive loan provider typically does not receive any kind of equity7 stake in capital future worth beyond their pre-determined rates of interest, yet there are no unalterable guidelines when it concerns personal resources. Typically private money is financed by one financier. These lendings are additionally frequently made use of when you believe you can raise the value of the home over a brief period of time, so you can handle the debt from that private money, refinance the residential property after adding value, as well as repay the exclusive lender. Much like with difficult money - exclusive cash should simply be made use of when you have numerous, plainly identified exit approaches.

If you are attempting to construct relationships for personal resources, developing credibility is a MUST. Whether it's through blogging regarding your real estate ventures on the internet, posting your property updates on Facebook, talking about real estate investing in table talk, or attending your regional realty financial investment club - you have to be visible. Are you maximizing your presence? Are you creating opportunities to highlight your investing journey to others? You do not should be a show-off, however next.

time someone asks just what's new in your life, share a

few details of your real estate undertakings. You never recognize exactly what may come about.

Home Equity Loans and Lines of Credit –

Lots of investors choose to tap into the equity7 in their own main the home of aid fund the investment of their investment residential properties. Financial institutions as well as various other lending institutions have numerous various items, such as a Home Equity7 Installment Loan (HEIL) or a Home Equity7 Line of Credit (HELOC) that enable you to take advantage of the equity7 you've currently acquired. As an example, an investor might purchased a property7, however instead of looking at the normal problem of trying to finance the investment property7 itself - they can as an alternative secure a HELOC on their own the home of spend for the property7.

In order to acquire a home equity7 loan or line of credit - you need to first have equity in your home. Banks will typically simply lend up to a particular percent of your home's value - in total. This percentage varies in between lenders, but it is not unusual to discover a lending institution that will certainly supply to lend as much as 90 % of the value of your residence.

Real World Example:

John's present residence is worth $100,000. John sees with his neighborhood financial institution and finds out that they will allow up to 90 % financial obligation on that particular home. Consequently, John can borrow a total amount of $90,000 on the house.

If he currently owes $50,000 on a very first home mortgage - the house equity line or loan would be capped at $40,000 to ensure the overall lendings didn't exceed 90 %.

Utilizing residence equity loans and also credit lines have a number of perks over typical fundings, including:.

Loan is based upon the worth of your key house - not the newly acquired property. This implies that the financial institution that is giving the loan won't generally even look at the new home. They do not usually worry themselves with just what your intent is with the money - just your capacity to pay it back. Thus, the brand-new residential property can be in horrible disorder and also the mortgage lender most likely won't care.

When you have a residence equity financing or line - the cash is your own to do with exactly what you really want. It's not depending on the brand-new property - so you can supply "Cash" when making offers on new properties and also therefore, you will certainly have a higher opportunity of getting your deals approved. Residence equity lines and also lendings might have specific tax benefits, such as the capacity to deduct the interest paid on that loan, enabled by the IRS. View a certified CPA or attorney for additional information on this.

Due to the fact that the financing is safeguarded by your key home, the interest rate on home equity financings as well as lines is typically really low as compared to tough cash or personal cash. To find out more concerning what existing rates are on these products, check out the BiggerPockets Mortgage Center.

An additional method frequently utilized by investors is to utilize a small bit of their home equity to fund the deposit on their assets home.

Real World Example:.

Sarah, a financier, wants to acquire an investment residential property for $100,000 - yet does not have any kind of extra down payment. She does, however, have a bunch of readily available equity in her own main home (she owes $50,000 however the home is worth $100,000.) Sarah opens up a $20,000 house equity financing on her personal the home of locate the down payment and afterwards obtain a conventional home loan from a mortgage lender for the remaining $80,000 on the financial investment home.

Finally - home equity loans as well as lines had both taken care of and modifiable rate of interest. Make certain to look at your goals, time-tables, and also monetary position when determining which house equity item you intend to make use of to more your investing profession.

Partnerships

We touched briefly on the use of "partners" in chapter four - however one more part of that discussion that we really did not discuss is their capability that can help you finance a bargain. If you intend to invest in a piece of residential property, but the price array is outside of your pocketbook - an equity partner could be a welcome addition to your team. An equity companion is somebody that you bring right into a deal in order to help finance the property. Collaborations can be structured in numerous various ways, from using a companion's money to finance the entire home, to utilizing a companion to simply money the down payment. There are no collection "regulations" with equity partnerships - however each situation and also bargain needs it's very own analysis of how the offer will certainly be assembled, which makes the decisions, and how earnings will be split at the end.

Depending upon the operating arrangement signed by both celebrations, the equity partner may have a current or passive part in the residential property. The ownership risk provided by the equity companion could enable that companion to definitely participate in almost all aspects of home possession. Furthermore, as a partner, they typically get, according to their possession percent, a return on their assets that includes cash flow, appreciation, depreciation, and also eventual revenue w7hen the residential property is sold.

Unlike a private lending institution, an equity partner does not get a decideded upon interest rate on their money. Instead, they obtain only a percentage of just what the residential property creates. If it makes a great deal of money then, their return will be higher, however if the assets sheds money, they might have to contribute money to maintain the residential property afloat. Equity companions take a greater risk than a personal lender might, yet in return they have the possibility of making

considerably a lot more when the investment is successful. Also, unlike in private lending - the equity companion's assets is not protected by a mortgage or cosigned
promissory note yet by an operating contract in between the companions.

Business Loans

While the majority of the above options concentration largely on the household side of loans, the globe of commercial lending might likewise be viable choice for your investing. As a matter of fact, if you are planning to buy a home besides a one to four device house - an advertisement funding is possibly precisely what you'll be needing.

Advertisement loans typically have sightly greater rates of interest and fees, along with much shorter terms and also different certifying criteria. Worldwide of residential borrowing, the income of the customer is valued over almost every other location; industrial borrowing, nevertheless, is much more concentrated on the home rather. The logic behind this is straightforward: if you own a ten million buck apartment house and points fail - you aren't visiting have the ability to make that mortgage repayment if you make $20,000 each year or $200,000 annually in personal earnings.

The advertisement loan provider will still look at your revenue, credit rating, and other personal economic indicators however just to get a photo as to your abilities financially. What's more important in the vast bulk of cases, is the quantity of profits a property creates.

Additionally, commercial lenders could commonly prolong a "business line of credit" to fund turns or other investments. Some financiers have the ability to get a huge "business line of credit rating" which allows them access to cash money for home flipping as well as other real estate endeavors.

EIULS, Life Insurance, ROTH IRAs, and Other Sources

There a wide range of various other assets as well as cost savings products around that you could make use of to purchase realty. While we do not have the time to cover each of these in detail, be sure to talk with a certified financial advisor regarding methods that you could make use of these products in your investing job.

Moving On

As you can see, there are many different means you could fund an assets property. One of one of the most valuable roles you play as a financier is in your capacity to locate creative ways to regularly move on with your assets. As every offer is various from one another, you will find yourself using lots of various financing methods throughout your job - so being able to recognize the different choices will certainly assist you throughout your entire investing journey.

An additional useful, and equally important, duty you will certainly be playing as a financier is the part of marketing specialist. Chapter seven will certainly take a look at the concept of property advertising in detail and also will provide you ideas and approaches to use to supercharge your investment chances. Advertising is necessary not simply for acquiring residential properties, yet additionally for selling as well as leasing

Chapter 6:
Real Estate Marketing

- Regardless of what element of real estate investing you opt to take part in, you will most likely should make use of marketing in some fashion. Advertising is the process of getting to outdoors your regular sphere of influence to push your company forward. Where you take your business is.

- In this chapter you'll learn: totally depending on you and your advertising and marketing abilities.

- Your Greatest Marketing Tool: Yourself.

- Marketing Through Networking.

- Networking in the Online World.

- Your Marketing Funnel.

- Marketing Through Direct Mail.

Your Greatest Real Estate Marketing Tool: Yourself

As a real estate investor - the initial and also crucial point yo u'll be advertising and marketing is yourself - your very own personal brand name. It does not take a bunch of cash, as well as it does not take a bunch of time. You will begin developing a brand name around on your own the moment that you start talking with others about property. You never ever recognize where these conversations are visiting lead you - so safeguard your brand increasingly. Allow's look a little further at the best ways to properly market your very own personal brand.

Be Honest

As a brand-new investor - you are not visiting recognize every little thing which's 100 % fine. One of the quickest means to tarnish your reputation is when you begin speaking about points that you do not actually understand much concerning. When you try to come off as an "professional"as well as you're not one, various other real financiers will recognize right away and also will not squander any time taking care of you. Admit just what you have no idea as well as utilize that to learn.Infact, among the most effective means to increase as a business owner is to ask a bunch of concerns and also, in humility, hear those who want to teach.

Additionally - don't mis-represent on your own. We often see new financiers do this right here on BiggerPockets and also elsewhere online. Just what you'll often view, is a new financier emerging and introducing themselves as such. Then, in just a couple of days (occasionally much less) they discuss having "properties in all 50 states" that they want to sell on price cut. Unless that person instantly acquired dozens of homes over night - that individual is most likely mis-representing themselves. Most of the times, that person is simply a wholesaler complying with the suggestions of a guru somewhere and also attempting to construct a customers listing for their future bargains. Yes, constructing a buyers listing is surprisingly vital. Doing so under false- pretenses, nevertheless, is the surest method to never negotiate.

You'll likewise locate brand-new financiers marketing offers by means of Craigslist or various other websites, yet these are deals that they have no interest in. Like in the previous example, these individuals are existing concerning deals to obtain various other investors which may be curious about them. If you obtain broken lying concerning a deal, you could rest assured that you'll never work with those individuals who discover it.

Integrity

Do you do exactly what you state you will do? Your integrity is the important things that will keep folks returning to collaborate with you, over and over again. As an investor, your credibility and reputation will precede you any place you go. This means that you need to continuously make certain you are showing the highest degree of integrity7. Imagine a loan provider who vows to provide however then backs out at the last 2nd - would certainly they continue to grow their business? Just how about a property agent that damages his business owners and swoops in on all the good deals under his business owner's feet - would he remain to increase his brand? Your honesty is an integral part of your brand - and also can quickly be tarnished. Maintain the highest specifications of stability and business will discover you.

Professionalism

Are you intending on running a hobby or a company?

If you wish to be seen as a business expert, you can start right now. Eveiy decision you make, eveiy partnership you construct, as well as eveiy product you get: be professional. You do not should be a million dollar company to resemble one. Appearing to a house with an unclean hawaiian shirt and shorts most likely isn't visiting give you the expert graphic you want to be successful. The same opts for the business cards you order, the voicemail on your phone, and the look of your car. People count on professionals - so begin imitating one.

Real Estate Marketing Through Networking

Among one of the most crucial marketing techniques you could start carrying out today is by networking. Networking is just the procedure of being familiar with others for the objective of relocating both individuals forward. It does not need to a formal thing - but your daily interactions should be part of your networking method. Networking is frequently considered occurring at an event, where lots of people get together as well as socialize, exchange cards and also tell market specific tales. While yes, this is a kind of networking (frequently seen at market certain meetings and also conferences) networking is actually a way of life.

Some of the most notable connections you'll make will certainly come from unplanned discussions about your realty investing. I'm not recommending that you just walk up to complete strangers and also begin telling them about your dreams and objectives - however take advantage of discussing your business when the chance emerges. You'll be amazed at the amount of people have an interest in realty and also exactly how frequently one fast mention of realty brings about a whole chat.

Not only is networking important for meeting individuals and companies that can move your company ahead - it's also effective for developing your property group (which we covered thoroughly in chapter four). No person could be successful completely on their own - so locating the best individuals to collaborate with is just one of the crucial jobs you can do at the start.

Speaking of crucial, one of one of the most important places you can begin networking at is your regional real estate investing club. Situated in almost every major city, individuals collect at these clubs on a regular basis to talk about existing market fads and investing strategies, to swap tenant horror tales, as well as to make connections. Many of the most essential folks on your team will most likely come from your local assets club. Realty assets clubs can vary considerably in dimension as well as quality - so if there are multiple clubs in your city - be sure to inspect them full blast. For a listing of regional real estate financial investment clubs, view the BiggerPockets Real Estate Clubs page.

Do remember that numerous of these clubs are also made to be earnings centers for their owners. So, you might have to endure sales pitches from masters as well as various other salespeople. That said, there is nothing more vital compared to connecting with your regional peers, and also these clubs area an excellent area to locate them.

There are various other networking events that are

excellent for fulfilling your peers, consisting of property owner association conferences, meetups, as well as small real-time occasions arranged by your peers right here on BiggerPockets.

- A final note on networking: get yourself some.
- professional business cards. While several facets of "old time" advertising and marketing are fading away - the business card continues to be a staple in the realty market. Make sure that your business card has the following details:.
- Your Name.
- Your Company Name.
- Your Company Position Title.
- Your Website.
- Your Phone Number.
- Your Email Address.
- Your Wants/Needs if Applicable (We Buy Houses).

Networking in the Online World

The globe is altering a lot more digital each day - as well as to be a leading entertainer in the realty spending industry you are going to need to change likewise. Let's check out a few locations you could begin networking online:

BiggerPockets.com- BiggerPockets is an on the internet community of realty professionals that network with each other daily, all the time, that can help each other discover, expand, and succeed. Start your networking right here. It is important to note that when networking with others, it is not regarding "just what can I leave it" but instead "how can I contribute to the discussion.".

Socialize on our forums, asking inquiries when needed, and answering others when you can. Discuss post, send coworker requests, adhere to prominent customers, as well as involve whenever possible. Networking on BiggerPockets is the same as networking in the real world - it's not a one-time point. Look for to come to be an acquainted (as well as friendly) face on the website. This indicates to make sure you have a picture posted to your profile - which your profile is totally filled in. Would certainly you wish to network with someone which had no face to relate to and you had no suggestion what their stoiy was? Never. Relationships are constructed with count on, as well as rely on is built through transparency. For more info on acquiring involved, as well as for url valuable tutorials, look into our Start Here page.

Your Website -Having an internet site suggests professionalism in the sector - a type of "online store front" to your company. That store needs to look welcoming, expert, as well as tidy in order to bring in folks. In today's tech-friendly globe - a great internet site is not difficult or costly to construct, even if you are horrible at modern technology.

Social Media - Facebook, Twitter, LinkedIn, Google+, and dozens of various other social media networks are available and also are ripe for networking. You don't have to have a presence on every single network, but concentrating on one or two is far better compared to being non-existent on all them. The technique to networking using social media, however, is to not utilize it as an advertising and marketing platform. Social network is about developing partnerships, so invest your time developing strong relationships and also make a name on your own as someone with knowledge.

Writing a blog - A blog is just an online collection of short articles, gotten from latest to oldest. A blog site can assist you develop reputation' in your investing area however can also be a fantastic tool for ironing out your ideas on paper (well, on the screen) and also hashing out suggestions. Furthermore, blogging can be a fun way to return to the neighborhood. If you have an interest in holding your very own real estate blog site, you could sign up for a totally free blog precisely BiggerPockets.

Your Marketing Funnel

Advertising and marketing funnels are created to transition an individual from having no knowledge concerning your company to the point where they are ready to engage in a business relationship with you. Folks utilize advertising funnels in nearly every form of company, and also realty investing is no different.

You are possibly aware of a "channel" - typically used for pouring large amounts of fluid right into a small area, such as putting oil in a car. At the top - the funnel is at it's widest, gathering the most total of whatever material you are capturing. As the compound moves down the funnel, it obtains smaller sized as well as smaller till it appears the bottom right into whatever container you are pouring it into. Similarly - your advertising funnel will seek to bring in one of the most amount of individuals on top, and also with progressive steps your channel will get even more particular up until you have a much smaller number of people left to create your wanted goal.

The sort of marketing funnel you established will certainly depend considerably on the sort of spending you get involved in. An advertising channel for a wholesaler is going to be considerably various compared to that of a note customer - however probably with comparable styles. For example – a wholesalers funnel might look a lot such as this:.

- Send out postcards to people that are unpaid on their home loan.
- Set up a 1-800 voicemail number for folks to ask for repossession help.
- Allow individuals to leave a voicemail if they want even more information concerning selling their home.
- Call people that left a message and screen for possible excellent leads.
- Meet with the excellent leads as well as make deals.
- Get deals accepted and authorize an investment and also sale contract.
- Do due diligence.
- Close on the residential property.

Notification that in each action, the channel narrows. At the start, maybe 5 thousand individuals receive mailers.

From them, possibly just a hundred individuals make the call to the number on your postcards. From that hundred, simply twenty leave a voicemail, of which simply 4 warrant an individual see and also a deal. Ultimately, maybe 1 or 2 of those deals could actually result in an authorized bargain for the wholesaler.

While it might seem like a radical waste - that people or 2 deals could cause a substantial monetary windfall for the wholesaler. This is simply one example of a functional advertising funnel. As stated over - your advertising and marketing funnel may vary a fair bit from the above funnel.

As an investor, you should be continuously determining and also tweaking your marketing funnel. You can and also need to examine your funnel to continually raise conversions-- the portion of individuals who make it right through the funnel to your desired end result.

For instance, (to draw from the wholesale channel example above) you could obtain two separate telephone number, split the team of past-due homeowners asunder, sending out half the postcards to one group and fifty percent to the various other - and gauge the results. Do you obtain more phone calls from postcard A or B? If postcard A received two times as numerous calls - then use that as your "baseline" as well as examine again with another postcard C. As you can see, your advertising and marketing funnel can continuously be modified, checked, and also determined to make it run like a well-oiled equipment.

Advertising Through Direct Mail.
Just what is Direct Mail?

While we are on the subject of postcards and also mailing letters, let's discuss that in more depth. This type of advertising and marketing is referred to as "direct mail." Direct mail is just the process of corresponding to targeted individuals via the mail, in hopes that a tiny portion will respond to those letters. Whether you are a wholesaler, flipper, or buy-and-hold investor - your company depends on locating great deals and having a consistent supply of leads for those bargains. Direct-mail advertising can be a wonderful device for building a steady supply of leads for your company, as well as can be a terrific way to maintain your funnel full. For several financiers - it is their primary source of leads.

How does Direct Mail Work?

Direct mail projects are designed to construct understanding of your product or service over time. Reflect to among the remaining acquisitions you made, such as a beverage at Starbucks, a movie you leased, or a track you purchased from iTunes. Possibilities are, you didn't purchase that product the initial time you read about it. Most individuals just don't buy from a business the very first time they find it. As a result, a direct-mail advertising campaign can not be a basic "one as well as done" project. By sending out messages over the course of time, the recipients end up being familiar with you as well as your service or product, and some will certainly respond as you become the solution to their requirements.

Exactly how do I Build a List to Send to?

You could build your list by making using of public records given by your local county assessor, or you can work with an on-line company like Listsource to obtain your listing for you. While using the pubic documents is totally free, using an online firm may save you time - so keep your goals in thoughts as you start producing your listing. Do note that you should have your listing re-done every 6 months or so to keep it fresh, as the market is constantly changing. You will certainly have to do away with those people that are no longer prospects for your certain list, and you will certainly would like to include in brand-new people.

What do I Send? There are 2 key options that financiers tend to send by mail to prospective leads. Allow's take a look at these briefly:

- Postcards - these can be either big or little, yet the advantage is that the recipient does not need to literally open an envelope to review exactly what's within.

- Yellow Letters - Written (or keyed in) on a real yellow notepad, these letters are typically mailed in an envelope. The reaction price is often very high, because of the "personal" nature of the letter.

Which Should I Send Direct Mail To?

Both the frequency with which you mail and the length of the project will certainly differ depending on the type of advertising and marketing channel you are establishing as well as the type of spending you are engaging in. Direct mail can be sent to basically anybody, so you'll need to look at your funnel and also decide. The following is a list of a few various types of individuals you might wish to target:

Absentee owners. For those aiming to obtain a large amount, those folks who are absentee owners are terrific targets, particularly those who endure of town. In a lot of cases these owners could have proposed job or an additional factor and could be planning to eliminate their home.

Deserted Properties. Folks could abandon a property for a range of factors - yet most of the times, they uncommitted sufficient regarding the residential property to wish to keep and also invest the money required to keep it up. Getting in touch with owners of homes that look to be shabby or abandoned could result in wonderful possibilities.

Probates. Probates are residential properties that are in the process of being distributed, in addition to the possessions of a departed person, to their heirs. When investors discuss probate investing, they are trying to find if a dead person had residential property, then tries to obtain the heirs/executor to offer that property to them at a price cut.

Pre-foreclosures and Foreclosures. People having problem with shedding their house are oftentimes highly encouraged to offer (however, often, they are highly anti-motivated and also opt to simply stick their heads in the sand.) You can many times locate a way to develop a "win win" situation to help these people conserve their credit rating as well as snag a great deal for yourself.

Apartment Owners. If you are looking to get into house purchasing, forwarding to apartment proprietors can be a wonderful way to stay on their radar. Your mailings do not have to be always targeted toward troubled or inspired vendors, but can be aimed towards individuals wTho want to fund the property' themselves utilizing vendor funding.

Expired Listings. Your realty broker will certainly have accessibility to all the residential properties on the MLS that did not market when specified with an agent. These individuals might be much more willing to cost a savings after their home was listed for time as well as didn't offer. In addition expired might likewise be inspired since they not should pay any type of real estate representative fees.Whatever particular niches you opt to work in, make certain to maintain organized documents of your campaigns, so you can measure and also check your outcomes, optimizing your initiatives.

Advertising and marketing Through Online Advertising

As an increasing number of folks invest their time online, you might be left behind if you don't relocate your property advertising right into that field as well. The internet offers many means you can market your real estate spending company, and - as with all advertising and marketing methods - the style of advertising you do depends substantially on the type of investing you participate in. The adhering to are a number of tools you could make use of to market online.

Facebook/Google Ads for Real Estate

Do you ever ask yourself how Facebook or Google make all their money? The majority of their income comes from their on the internet advertising platforms. As a financier - you can make use of these sources to target prospective sellers, customers, or various other company interactions. While Facebook as well as Google ads might look relatively similar, they differ in numerous essential means:

- Facebook enables you to target who views your advertisement based upon their passions, area, demographics, as well as connections on Facebook.
- Google allows you to target who sees your ad based upon their searches, web record, and also place.

The perk of these sort of online advertisements are that you could establish it up so you only pay when the ad functions.Think of asking a neighborhood newspaper to just charge you when somebody calls concerning your ad. There's no chance of that happening. Nonetheless, this is specifically what this sort of on-line marketing allows yon to do. This is known as "pay-per- click" advertising, meanings that you simply pay when a person clicks on an ad as well as visits your site. With pay-per-click marketing (such as ads on Facebook, Google, or Bing), you simply need to pay for the ad when your advertising campaign achieved it's objective of placing folks in your advertising funnel.

Benefits of Online Pav-Per-Click Advertising

- Most online pay-per-click advertisements allow you to be area specific - meanings that you can choose to have your advertising campaign viewed simply by people within 10, a hundred, or any type of number of miles of your defined area.

- Additionally, Facebook advertisements are passion particular. (Do you actually think Facebook's 'like" function is just for the user's benefit?) Facebook makes use of those "likes" and also relationship partnerships that can help marketers get to particular people. This implies, as a property online marketer, you can decide to show your advertisement only to individuals which have an interest in a certain subject.

- Finally, most pay-per-click advertising (specifically Facebook) is demographically particular so you can advertise to specific ages or genders. For instance, you could produce a well created advertising campaign to entice initial time homebuyers by deciding to promote only to folks between twenty-two and thirty-two that live within 10 miles of a residential property you are trying to market.

Exactly how Online Advertisement Pricing Works:.

"How a lot does it set you back?" is a more difficult inquiry that it might seem.Pay-per-click advertising and marketing rates are based upon an "auction," implying that advertisers "bid" on a rate to display their ad. Marketing experts then contend for either keywords or passions, based on the requirements you are targeting your marketing to. When you established a new ad, you will tell Facebook, Google or Bing what price per click you wish to pay, as well as you'll usually never be charge you more than that. If you bid as well reduced - your advertisement will certainly not be revealed as a result of various other marketing experts paying more. The good news is, the significant pay-per-click companies do give a basic range of costs, so you can figure out the amount of you'll have to invest to reach a certain group. You likewise have the option to set a daily or month-to-month budget plan - so you can manage just how much you would like to spend on your advertising and marketing.

Recommendation for Creating Online Ads:
Where Will Your Ad Send People?

This location could be your very own website, your company Facebook web page, or any sort of site that you want. Just make sure this location is part of your marketing "channel."

Create a Title that Pops.

You are allowed just a minimal number of personalities

for your title - so make them attract attention. It is helpful when promoting to neighborhood capacities to make use of something neighborhood in the title to make the advertisement attract attention. On-line customers are not typically used to viewing local people and also put on an on-line advertisement - so ads like that often pop.

Interest them with your ad's body.

The part of the ad that is not the title is referred to as the "body." Interesting both reality as well as feeling when you create the copy for your ad's body can help triggering interest in both sides of the brain as well as boost clicks.

Advertise advantages over functions.

Use an Eye-Catcliing Photo.

If making use of Facebook - the photograph is the most crucial section of your ad since it is usually the only point audiences pay much focus on in the beginning. Catch their eye with the photo, which leads them to the title, which causes the physical body, which leads to clicks. An advertisement, in itself, is a channel also

Identify Your Price.

To prevent huge spending, be sure to establish your budget. Determine what your month-to-month or day-to-day budget plan is and quote on your advertisement cost. Display the results and adjust your proposal rate higher if you are not spending your total budget.

Split-test.

Split testing is the procedure of creating a number of advertisements, each with small modifications, to determine the best reaction rate from somebody taking a look at the ad. This is the same process we stated earlier when talking about sending different direct-mail advertising postcards to different teams.

Developing a Website or Landing Page.

A web site is not a need in order to catch leads, yet can be highly beneficial. Some investors just utilize a telephone number to gather leads, however having an internet site provides an additional opportunity to collect those prospective chances. If you don't have the technical expertise to produce a professional looking web site, make use of a pre-made design template from a site like Wix.com or just work with a freelancer at a site such like Odesk.com, eLance.com. or Designs.com to develop the site for you. You could likewise create a Facebook company web page that completes your goal, yet haring your marketing channel by yourself website does provide you a lot more control.

For additional information on Marketing and producing an advertising and marketing funnel, view Using Facebook Advertising to Supercharge Your Real Estate Marketing.

Moving On

As you could view, realty advertising and marketing is not a simple procedure. Each of the categories pointed out above could be expanded upon significantly and also an entire book could be mitten about each. We additionally did not cover eveiy alternative available, yet those that we really feel to be the most commonly made use of today. The important thing when just starting is to focus on one or two advertising and marketing strategies, as well as to execute them carefully, while checking the results. Once you discover something that works, stay with it, and if you intend to create more leads, increase it or move on to one more advertising and marketing technique. In the same way - not all advertising approaches are going to produce reliable outcomes. This is why preserving exact records and also regularly testing your marketing campaigns is essential.

Up until this factor, we have actually considered how you can choose your assets method and niche, how to plan for your following assets, the best ways to fund your home, and also how to make use of advertising to make it all take place. In the next chapter, we are going to consider the method you actually begin making lots of money from your assets: performing your exit technique.

DISCLAIMER AND/OR LEGAL NOTICES:

Made in the USA
San Bernardino, CA
11 January 2016